LANGUAGE FOR THE PRESCHOOL DEAF CHILD

Language

for the Preschool

Deaf Child

By Grace Harris Lassman

Teacher of the Deaf; formerly Instructor of Speech,
John Tracy Clinic, Los Angeles, California

Forewords by Dr. S. R. SILVERMAN
and Mrs. HARRIET MONTAGUE

1 9 5 0

GRUNE & STRATTON

New York

Library of Congress Catalog Card No. 50–10170

TO

the parents and deaf children whom I have taught and who have
helped to make this book helpful to other parents and deaf children

C O N T E N T S

Part II Activities for Language Development

Part III The Nursery School for Deaf Children and Parent Education

Foreword

by S. R. SILVERMAN, PH.D.

Director, Central Institute for the Deaf; Pro-
fessor of Audiology, Washington University,
St. Louis, Missouri.

For the relatively small number of individuals who comprise
our profession of educating the deaf we are by tradition amaz-
ingly vehement about our differences of opinion concerning
the proper manner in which we must discharge our professional
obligations. Such classical issues as manual vs. combined vs. oral
methods, the day vs. the residential school, and "analytic"
methods vs. "natural" methods of teaching speech are still hotly
debated. But one point on which we have reached almost uni-
versal agreement is that *language is the keystone upon which*
successful education of the deaf ultimately rests. It is with this
language problem that Mrs. Lassman comes to unusually effective grips at a critical stage in the child's development.

We are all aware of the relatively rapid mental, physical, psychological and social growth which takes place in the so-called
preschool period in a child's life. Mrs. Lassman recognizes the
potentialities for effective learning in these early years. She
makes available a rich storehouse of sound advice and practical
procedures which enable not only the teacher but also the parent to take full advantage of the young deaf child's tractability.
Furthermore, the material assists the parent in gaining an in-

structive appreciation of the child's problems of communication which is frequently difficult for the layman to grasp.

Mrs. Lassman's book is particularly timely. In our latter day concern for psychological and auditory assessment and diagnosis through various testing techniques, we seem to have attenuated our interest in practical educational techniques to the point where the testing fringe is getting larger than the teaching cloth. This trend, fortunately, has not been without its significant value. It has led to early detection and assessment of the deaf child and consequently to wider acceptance of the value of instruction at the preschool level.

Now we need to have increasingly effective teaching procedures to meet these instructional needs. Mrs. Lassman's creative mind, nurtured by her own rich experience and that of her predecessors and contemporaries, has met the challenge superbly.

Above all, Mrs. Lassman conveys to her readers a spirit of rational hope and optimism about the worthwhileness of our efforts on behalf of the deaf child. To the parent in particular, what could be a more constructive contribution?

Foreword

by HARRIET ANDREWS MONTAGUE

*Director and Editor, Correspondence Course
for Parents of Little Deaf Children, John
Tracy Clinic, Los Angeles, California.*

It has been my privilege to watch this book grow. I have seen it grow on paper, and I have seen it grow in the flesh, as the author worked out, in daily contacts with little deaf children and their parents, the methods she outlines here in such clear detail.

It is a rare experience to watch her teach, for, like all good teachers, she has an intuitive knowledge of *what* to do. Moreover, with her capacity for intellectual analysis, she understands better than most teachers the *why* of what she does. And because she knows both the *what* and the *why,* she is admirably equipped to write a book for the guidance of teachers and parents of deaf children, as well as for other individuals who at one time or another must deal with the problems of deafness.

I can say without exaggeration that she is an inspired teacher of speech to the deaf. There is not one statement in this book, not one suggestion in regard to the development of speech and language that she has not proved through actual experience with small children. Nothing here is invented or made up for the occasion; every episode, every illustration, every achievement deals with a flesh and blood child. And through the alchemy of her acute intelligence, Mrs. Lassman has been able to fuse all this experience and knowledge into a workable textbook.

Parents as well as teachers can use it to advantage, particularly those parents who have themselves taught their preschool deaf children at home by means of the home study program Mrs. Lassman mentions. I think this book provides an excellent complementary manual to that series of lessons.

For five years I have worked at the same nursery school where Mrs. Lassman gathered much of the data she has used in this book. For a year, she and I worked together advising parents of deaf children by correspondence, and we studied out together some of the answers to parental problems. I gained greatly during this association.

It is with deep satisfaction that I see this book published in the United States. The author is by birth a Canadian, but she is an American citizen, and American teachers of the deaf have been far too apt to follow Caroline Yale's famous observation that they were "too busy doing the thing to write about it." The good books on the education of the deaf have come to us from other countries, especially from England. Here at last is an American textbook, printed in America, and written by a young teacher, who has not only enough experience behind her to speak with authority, but enough years ahead of her to promise other works of value in this field.

Throughout a lifetime of acquaintance with workers in the education of the deaf, I have had contact with many of the pioneers. I knew Mary True and Sarah Fuller and Caroline Yale and Alexander Graham Bell and Harris Taylor and E.A. Gruver, and A.L.E. Crouter, F.W. Booth, and Anne Sullivan. There have been times when I have wondered whether all the great spirits who contributed to the oral education of the deaf in the United States are departing from our midst, leaving no worthy successors behind; but as I read this book, and as I think of some of the other young, courageous, devoted teachers like Grace Lassman, I can say to these pioneers with all honesty, Be at peace; the staff you laid down is in good hands.

Preface

This book has been written to provide further assistance for parents, for students, and for teachers, in the guidance of young deaf children.

It has been an outgrowth of my work with parents, with deaf children, and with hearing children. The original material consisted of hundreds of daily records of the children and parents, and of parents' questions and problems raised in classes, during consultations, and through correspondence. After many months of organizing and reorganizing the material, it took its present form.

The final organization and presentation were decided upon in view of the nature of the parents' questions and problems regarding their respective deaf children, and in view of my own experiences and convictions.

If we follow the development of young deaf children and work with their parents for a length of time, we soon realize that there remains a huge gap between our approach to the child as a personality and our approach to him as a deaf child. Even where the parents receive training, there are indications that the psychological orientation runs along one channel, the training in regard to the deafness along another. It is dangerously easy to forget that the deaf child is a human being with feelings when the special lesson gets under way. It is dangerously easy to interpret "guiding the deaf child as a child" as a signal to eliminate all special training. The teamwork which is supposed to exist between parents and teachers and other workers in the field must be more than "talk." When such teamwork does develop, the chances of bridging the gap between the personality of the child and his deafness will be greater.

We know perfectly well that deafness itself creates many real and difficult problems, and that many of the methods which have been in operation for years are irreplaceable. Nevertheless, if we are completely honest with ourselves and with one another, we must admit that there are many problems encountered in the guidance of young deaf children which can't be resolved by merely exposing the child to "lessons."

There is a need for the worker, parent, and teacher, to put a sincere effort into striking a balance between the needs of the child and the demands of his deafness. No doubt, many of us have been guilty of ignoring everything in a book except those parts that tell us "what" to do. The "how" too often becomes what seems easiest for us at the moment.

An attempt has been made in this book to combine the "what" and the "how" in recognition of the child and the deafness. The parents of deaf children who may use this book are urged to read and reread the whole, before attempting to work with their respective children.

The material has been organized in such a way that it becomes more and more specific as it moves along. The introductory section includes a general, bird's-eye view of the problems created by deafness for the child, the parent, and the community.

Part I is concerned with the broad, fundamental aspects of the training, which must be understood before attempting to train the child.

Part II describes many activities which have been used successfully by teachers and parents in guiding deaf children at the preschool levels.

Part III includes a brief outline of the parent education program and nursery school for deaf children, record forms, and excerpts from the records of a few young deaf children.

The bibliography, which represents a cross-section of the literature pertinent to the guidance of the young deaf child, has been included in order to (1) substantiate statements made by the author; (2) to give credit where credit is due; (3) and to encourage the reader to explore the literature.

Although this book is addressed to parents, students, teachers, and all other individuals interested in the welfare of the deaf child, I am particularly concerned with the first group, the parents. Parents hold much more power in their hands than they sometimes realize, even while they may feel inadequate and in need of help. My experience with the parents of young deaf children has given me a strong faith in the adequacies and potentialities of parents in training and guiding their deaf children. They have already contributed much; they will contribute more. Their efforts are not futile. It is my hope that this book will give them additional hope and strength.

G.H.L.

Acknowledgments

It is impossible to list here the names of the many individuals to whom I am indebted. Such a list would have to include those who have shared and discussed professional problems and achievements with me from the beginning of my professional work; whose literature has been a constant source of inspiration and help. The list must be confined to those individuals who have contributed most directly to this book.

I extend my deepest appreciation to:

Harriet Montague, for her encouragement, her interest, her suggestions and criticisms. She gave much of her valuable time to reading and editing the material. The final reorganization of the material makes it impossible to indicate the specific sections, paragraphs, and sentences which felt the touch of Mrs. Montague. I regret that there is not more evidence of her literary talent. It has been a great pleasure to have been associated with and encouraged by Mrs. Montague, whose years of notable contribution to the education of the deaf cannot be adequately honored.

Mary E. Numbers, for the time and attention she gave to the material when it was still in skeleton form. Her suggestions and cogent criticisms of the first draft remained helpful throughout the writing.

Virginia Guthrie Lee, for the pleasure of working with her, and of watching her "discover the child" as few people are capable of doing.

Catherine Ford, for her guidance and her standards and human qualities in working with deaf children and teachers.

Mrs. Spencer Tracy, for the opportunity of working and learning in John Tracy Clinic, which she directs; and for permission to use the photographs which were taken in that center.

James Madden, Black Starr Studios, Los Angeles, California, for taking and contributing most of the photographs in this book.

Dr. Victor Goodhill, otologist, for assistance in publishing.

My husband, *Frank Lassman,* for his continuous encouragement.

Juanita Spyres Wiley, Evelyn Anderson, Clifford Holmes, and the host of other professional associates from whom I have learned.

Introduction

Deafness in Childhood—

A Problem and a Responsibility

Deafness in Childhood — A Problem and a Responsibility

THE WHOLE AND THE PART

The family next door views deafness in the little child in one way, the parent sees it in another light; the teacher in another; the doctor in another. The deaf adult who has never learned to talk sees the child in an entirely different light from that in which the speaking deaf adult sees him. The psychologist, the research worker, and the scientist have their particular points of view. Whatever the ideas of these people may be, they are important in so far as they may affect the deaf child, at present and for the future, and deter or accelerate the ultimate development of our total society. Each of these individuals has a definite responsibility to the deaf child, and that responsibilty, regardless of the respective roles, can be assumed effectively only if there is a realization of the fact that all are working for or with a human being.

Educational techniques, hearing aids, tests and examinations, parent classes, and other facilities are important, and it is essential that the functioning of each be well understood and directed by experts. In the last analysis, however, to consider any one of these specialties apart from the *individual* for whom it is intended would be indeed an artificial operation.

Although the educator, the scientist, the doctor, the parent, the psychologist, the layman, and others have their own particular perspectives, and all find it necessary to expound theories, to analyze, to isolate certain factors, to consider deafness and the deaf child as entities apart from the world, the most productive attitude toward deafness and the problems it creates is to see the total situation, with the deaf child—the one who has to live with the deafness for the rest of his life—as the core of that situation.

If we can achieve this end, the particular section of the whole which needs special attention can be more easily recognized and successfully treated, since we are not only able to see it alone but in relationship to the whole.

The degree to which the worker—parent, teacher, or other—is able to hold true to this basis will determine his or her capacity to understand and meet the general and specific problems created by deafness.

THE DEAF CHILD'S PROBLEM

Every child has to face problems involved in his adjustment to the world as a whole, to the neighborhood society, and to the immediate environment into which he was born; [73] and the little deaf child has these same adjustments to make as well as many others contingent upon his deafness.[76]

The primary problems brought on by the deafness itself magnify or create environmental and social problems, and the latter increase and magnify the former.[15] Deafness, the parents, and the community are all problems for the child. Since the deafness tends to complicate and magnify the other problems, those problems most directly concerned with it should be recognized and understood.

Oral Communication

Chief among the handicaps caused by deafness is the difficulty in establishing a form of communication, essential to normal living. The fact that the little deaf child doesn't hear makes it

2

impossible for him to understand the spoken language of others, and since he does not understand this language he cannot speak it unless he is specially trained to do so.[10]

To the parent, as to other laymen, the chief problem seems to be lack of speech. "When will my child talk?" is among the first questions the parent asks, for the child's inability to speak is apparently the characteristic that makes him different from other children. Fortunately, as is now widely known by parents and society, though still not sufficiently so, *the deaf child can learn to talk*.[13]

A realization of the possibilities for speech in the deaf child must be accompanied by a recognition of a more basic factor, one that is essential for speech by anyone. That factor is an understanding of spoken language. A specialist in speech development can train even a very young deaf child to "say" every vowel and consonant in our language, and many words. But what that child is able to "say" represents wasted effort on his and his instructor's part unless he understands what he is saying, feels a need and a desire to say it, knows when to say it, and can understand it when other people say it.[72]

The educator's cry to the parent is "understanding before speech." The hearing child is exposed to spoken language for months before he begins to talk, in spite of being in the fortunate position of having normal hearing. It takes him all that time to learn to understand what people are talking about and to discover that speech is a desirable tool for him.[171] The deaf child must be given the same opportunity to understand spoken language.

His eyes have to learn to do, alone, the job that the eyes and ears of the hearing child do. For this reason, the deaf child needs more time; how much more depends on the personality of the individual child, the age at which training was begun, and the success of the role his parents play in his development.[205]

Parents

If the deaf child is a problem to his parents, the parents most certainly may be a problem for the child. Teachers, doctors, and the neighbors, all have some influence on every child. But since the parents are the ones who live with the child day after day through good moments and bad, they are the ones whose continuous influence tends to be the greatest force in the child's life.[86] It might be said that this is especially true in the case of a handicapped child.

If the deaf child, or any child for that matter, could anticipate what life holds for him and what its demands on him would be, he would want to choose with care the individuals whose guidance during the early years would influence his future life.[219] Since this choice cannot be his, and since he cannot control the forces in the environment in which he finds himself, the adults in that environment, primarily his parents, have the responsibility of formulating his future by what they do in the present.[65]

The parent who can say to her deaf child, "I love you just as you are," with affection and sincerity, is not a problem to her child and will not handicap him further.[19] That parent will find a way to cope with the real problem—the deafness—and will win for herself and for her child a victory over the handicap.

There is, however, the parent who cannot accept her child as a deaf child. She may care for certain needs such as food, rest, special instruction, etc., but the very fact that a child of hers could be handicapped may prevent her accepting him completely.[149] The situation may be obvious or it may be so well cloaked that no one can detect a flaw unless the child were studied.[150] Such children have parent problems and so are doubly handicapped.[216]

Studies have revealed that many emotional problems of the deaf adolescent and adult, socially, academically, and vocationally, have their roots in their parents' attitudes towards the handicap.[33] Other studies reveal (through study of dreams) that although consciously the deaf persons express desires for more friends, more love, for power, for greater intelligence, and for adventure, their most powerful unconscious desire is to hear and to speak, since that would enable them to have more of what the hearing person apparently has—love, friends, achievement, and security.[192, 193, 194]

Evidently many deaf children, consciously or unconsciously, feel cheated of something vital to them, and something in their history has caused them to relate their deprivations to the deafness.[174]

However deeply the deaf child may want to hear and his parents want him to hear, he cannot gain normal hearing, and he will increasingly withdraw from people, from normal living, and from educational opportunities that could make him a happy member of society, unless his parents, through their own acceptance of him as he is and through the help they seek out, can aid him to develop inner feelings of security and to acquire early in life the tools for accepting his handicap and adjusting to society.[133]

The parents' attitude towards the handicap must be one of acceptance, so that the child too will be able to accept it and, looking at it with a certain amount of objectivity, will not have to be content with a dream of achievement but may achieve in fact.[84]

The deaf child's morale needs to be reinforced by healthy attitudes early in life if he is to develop as normally as possible. The environment provided for him by his parents has a definite and lasting bearing on his adjustment to the world and even on his capacity to choose wisely a vocation which he can follow efficiently and which will nourish in him a feeling of contribution and success.[28]

The deaf child can learn to understand spoken language and to talk. The success with which he can do this will depend to a

5

great extent on the nature of the parent problems which surround him, about which he can do nothing, but which inevitably affect him.[17]

The Community

The neighbors, the school, the church, the doctor, the dentist, and all those other people who make up a community can present additional problems to the deaf child, or they may be among the greatest supports in his life. There are still many people who do not exhibit enough interest in the handicapped child either to ask questions or to listen to explanations. Nevertheless, since many of these people come in contact with the deaf child, an effort must be made to reach them.

Some individuals view deafness or any other physical handicap as a contagious disease, and such an attitude affects the child both directly and indirectly. The deaf child's mother is hurt and her resources further undermined, every time the woman next door speaks of the child as "deaf and dumb," or "the dummy." The mother's feelings, which are more normal than abnormal under the circumstances, affect her relationship with her deaf child.[200]

The handicap of deafness is less obvious to the casual observer than other physical handicaps such as blindness and paralysis. This may sometimes be an advantage, but it may sometimes baffle and frighten the person who has had no contact with deafness, with frequent results of thoughtless, harmful, and even cruel behavior towards the child.

Mrs. Winters who learns that Mrs. Brown's child is deaf grimaces, shakes her head in pity or horror, remembers a deaf boy she encountered when she was very young and recalls the signs he used, the unpleasant sounds he made, the fact that people felt sorry for him and didn't bother with him except to humor him occasionally. Mrs. Winters can only pity Mrs. Brown and the child—and never realizes that the picture she has conjured up out

6

of her one experience with a deaf person could be a detrimental force in the child's whole life! Her one experience may make her feel informed about the subject, and her regrettable attitude towards the child may spread throughout the community.

The preschool deaf child who is getting instruction in the home by the parent or a tutor needs experiences with other children, especially with hearing children. The parent may try to have the child accepted in a nursery school for hearing children and, as has often happened, the child is rejected by the school on the basis of objections by the hearing children's parents, through lack of understanding on the part of the educators.

To educate the child only in the schoolroom sense, forgetting the world into which he must take his place, is to limit the special education and to handicap the child further.

It would be a great mistake to denounce the community for its "errors." In a sense the community has been the forgotten group where the handicap of deafness is concerned. It must be educated so that people like Mrs. Winters will spread the right kind of information, and prove to be a help, not a hindrance, to the deaf child.

THE PARENTS' PROBLEM

Every parent encounters problems in guiding a child through childhood. Parents of the deaf child have a more serious problem. They did not wish for a deaf child any more than the child wanted to be born deaf or to become deaf after birth. This unappointed and unexpected blow cannot help but change the course of the parents' lives for good or otherwise.

The first problem very likely arises when the parent begins to suspect that there is "something wrong" with the child. Probably it will be only after days and weeks of wary observation and worry that the suspicion centers upon the possibility of defective hearing.

Possibly the period between suspecting deafness and having

7

the suspicion confirmed is one of the most frightening, emotional periods for both parents. Most parents have little if any knowledge of deafness and of what can be done for the deaf child. Consequently, they may have visions of their child going through life unable to speak, different from others, a stigma to them socially, or a lifelong burden to them since they think that he will be capable of doing only the most menial of jobs. They may feel that they are being punished for something, feel guilty, develop suspicions about each other. Certainly they are unhappy.[206]

In most cases, the parents consult the family physician or an otologist.[137] The suspicion may be confirmed immediately, or, as has happened, the parents may be forced to travel from office to office, sometimes from city to city. They may get a number of opinions, which add to the problem. Or, in spite of getting the same statement from each doctor, they may refuse to face the facts and continue to search for some person who will tell them what they want to hear—that the child is perfectly normal. The parent who does this is heaping problems upon herself and her child.[208]

What is happening to the child as he is taken from specialist to specialist, in the midst of this turmoil of unhappy feelings? Is the parent really thinking of the child, or is she seeking relief for herself? Such parents must be reached and helped.[201]

The medical person whom the parents contact can be a force for good in the life of both parent and child, or he can be another complication of the problem. More and more medical people are able to recognize deafness, and will refer the parent to a competent otologist. The otologist will diagnose the situation and advise the parent to apply to a center for educational guidance, either locally or by correspondence or both. Unfortunately, there are still instances of a parent being told that all she can do is "wait" until the child is of school age, when he can be sent away.

Fortunate indeed is the parent who discovers the deafness

while the child is very young, gets reliable direction regarding educational possibilities for herself and her deaf child, and can start the training at once.[139]

But the parents' problems do not end immediately upon the discovery of deafness in the child, enrolment in parents' classes in a guidance center, and arranging for nursery school and home training for the child. If *both* parents assume responsibility for their deaf child in every possible way, and reach out eagerly for all the information and guidance they can get, problems which are bound to arise can be resolved in great degree by the parents.

On the other hand, one or the other of the parents, or both, may refuse to take an active part in the education and guidance of their child. Their feelings of inadequacy may make them hostile towards the very instructors to whom they want to shift all the responsibility. The relief some parents feel when they discover that the child can be trained to understand language and to speak is often replaced by feelings of anxiety, apathy, and possibly downright weariness or even annoyance that they must still take an active part in the development of their child's speech and language.[218]

These feelings and attitudes are problems for the parents and, in turn, become problems for the child. Condemnation and harsh criticism of the parents will not solve the problem for either child or parent.[93] Neither will eliminating the parent from participation in the child's education solve the problem.[96]

Aside from emotional problems, the parent encounters many very real ones. She has the community to cope with. Her child needs other children, and it is her task to try to get the understanding of the people around her. Children do have their good and bad moments, but if the parents of the children in the neighborhood can be reached, then the squabbles and differences among the children can be held down to everyday ones, and will not be those in which the deaf child is constantly made "the

9

goat," or the target of abuse, or a cause for pity and lack of respect as a human being, or the one who stands alone.

There is the parent whose child is ready to go to school. Possibly she lives near a school for deaf children whose methods and philosophy are contrary to those she has learned to accept and has found to be workable through her own training of the child. She may write away for information about other schools and find that there is a residential school, within the family means, where the child would get the kind of training she wants for him. The choice must be hers—whether to keep him at home and send him to the local school at a possible sacrifice, or to send him away at another sacrifice.

The parent may be able to interest the local school board in starting a day class for the deaf children in the community, based on the principles she believes to be most effective. She may fail in this attempt and be thrown back to the necessity of choosing between what she considers one imperfect situation or the other.

Many parents have been faced with such problems. Generally, the parent who has gone through the early years *with* her child, has given him every opportunity possible under existing circumstances, and has given some serious thought to the future schooling of the child, makes the wise choice.[135]

The real and psychological problems of the parents of the deaf child may be numerous or few. There are always some. To some degree they can be met. The solutions may not be "perfect" but can be satisfactory, conditioned only by geographical and financial factors, the kind of help available, and the kind of person the parent is.

THE COMMUNITY'S PROBLEM

The community, composed as it is of many kinds of people in different walks of life, with all of whom the deaf child has to learn to live, often presents a problem to parent and child, but also has its own problems in regard to the deaf child. Many of the people whose behavior seems cruel and stupid to the parents of the deaf child actually think that they are doing the "right" thing for the majority.

For example: The deaf child in the neighborhood has become a problem for the parents of the hearing children by *his being accepted* by the children. The parents may be afraid that their children will adopt some of the "peculiarities" of the handicap, that the friendship may continue into adulthood, and that in all fairness to their children they should do something to terminate. the relationships as soon as possible.

Or, there is Billy, the little deaf boy, playmate of Jimmy who hears. Jimmy takes Billy home with him and they go into the kitchen for some cookies. It doesn't seem to matter to Jimmy that Billy doesn't hear. The important thing to him is that Billy can do the things he likes to do and they have a lot of fun together. But Jimmy's mother, who can't see beyond the handicap, stands off from Billy even while she smiles and gives him a cookie. She feels so uncomfortable with this deaf child. What can she "say" to him? She feels downright silly talking to this child who doesn't hear what she says. Why in the world does Jimmy want to play with him? . . . If that mother isn't reached and given the right kind of information, her feelings and attitudes will be trans- ferred to her child, who will transfer them to other children in the neighborhood; and Billy, the deaf child, will be slowly ostra- cized.

There may be the teacher who is confronted by the parent who wants her deaf child to attend the nursery school for hearing children. She recognizes Billy as an alert-looking, attractive child. At the same time, she may withdraw from the idea of having a child *like that* in her class. She has so much to do as a teacher of so many hearing children, and this deaf child would add to her responsibility. She likes children, is a good teacher, is basically kind and interested in the welfare of the community, but after all she must think of the other children and the possible objec-

11

tions from their parents. In spite of all her rationalizations, how-ever, she is probably sincerely concerned.

Such situations and many others do arise in the community where the deaf child lives. If these people could be brought to understand that here is an opportunity, not only to do a great favor to one family, but to make a contribution to society as a whole, without any sacrifice on their part, and with little effort; if they could see that the "differences" and "peculiarities" of which they are afraid, are only as significant as they wish to make them; if they could be brought to see the child before the deaf-ness, the problem of the deaf child as far as they are concerned would be eliminated, and they would not be guilty of adding to the child's real handicap.

These are only some of the problems that arise for the deaf child, the parents, and the community. Those individuals who have worked with deaf children and their parents know that each set of circumstances surrounding each deaf child, his family, and his community presents its own particular problems, and that each must be dealt with individually.

Many of the problems have been coped with successfully, but far too many have not. The successful outcome depends on the motives, the degree of maturity, and the sense of responsibility of those persons who are in a position to lead the way.

EDUCATION AS A SOLUTION

It is fairly evident that the deaf child must be educated, the parent must be educated, and the community must be educated. No one person nor one group can do all that must be done and so there arises the question—

Who Educates Whom? When and Where?

The fact that the problems of deafness cannot be solved through education in the classroom nor by education of the child alone makes the task of those concerned much broader, more exacting as to training, personality, and responsibility, and more rewarding in terms of enjoyment and contribution. There is a great dearth of teachers qualified to train deaf children, parents, and students. Those who can get direct guidance must assume responsibility for finding and educating others. Those who know must tell those who don't, whenever the opportunity arises.

It is not necessary to know everything about deafness in order to help the deaf child, his parents, and members of the community. Just to pass along the information that the deaf child can be trained in language understanding and speech, that the training may be begun even in infancy,[121] and that the parents themselves may be educated in the guidance of their children, either by going to specific centers or through correspondence, is a valuable contribution.

The teacher, the parent, the individual in the community— each must assume a role and play it well. Every person must be permitted to do everything he is capable of doing, and one might venture to say that this is considerably more than has been permitted. No one of these people knows everything that can be known about deafness and the little child, and each is dependent on the others in some respect. This interdependence must be recognized if everything possible is to be done for the deaf child, especially during the first years which are so important.

How can a person contribute effectively, recognize his limitations, understand why he is more successful in one field than in another, or accept his responsibilities, unless he is taken into the situation wholeheartedly and given a picture of the *whole* problem and of the possibilities? [120]

There are difficulties and problems for all concerned. To gain the swiftest, most effective management of the difficulties and problems, training for the various skills should be placed in the hands of the "right" persons. The "right" person, however, is not the one who keeps "the bag of tricks" to himself, who is fearful of handing out information and intelligent guidance, or who will stand in the way of the parent's, the child's, the professional worker's, or the educational center's progress.

Where There Is No Teacher

After the parents have had a confirmation from the otologist concerning the deafness, their next thought must be in regard to a teacher who will guide them in training the child. If no such teacher is available in the community, the parent should know that there is available to her a correspondence course designed for use by other parents in precisely her situation: a course in the training of the preschool deaf child, which will be sent free of charge to any parent of a deaf child under five or six years of age, anywhere in the world.[135]

This course is not sent out in a body to the parent, for her to interpret and struggle along with, as best she can. It goes out in twelve monthly instalments, each instalment containing specific exercises which the parent may employ from month to month for the development of language understanding, speech, auditory training, lipreading, sense training, creative activities, and reading readiness. There are also many discussions of behavior problems which have helped hundreds of parents, all over the world, quite as much as have the specific exercises related to the handicap. The parent reports to the center each month by letter, writing details of what she has done, and about the child's responses. Each report is regarded as an individual matter and is answered personally.

The availability of this course should be made known ever more widely. Needless to say, training by correspondence has its limitations. It has been found, however, that the interest, the success—sometimes the failures—which have resulted from using this course, have often sent parents farther afield for personal guidance, have given them ideas of how to go about finding the right kind of personal help, have spurred parents into getting the interest of the community, and have been instrumental in the establishment of nursery school and preschool classes for young deaf children in many a community. Some parents who have had no other help than that available through correspondence have, by stimulating sufficient interest on the part of the public schools, obtained permission for a young deaf child to attend a hearing nursery or kindergarten.[212]

Parents of young deaf children should also take advantage of the facilities offered by the speech and hearing clinic in the nearest university.[124] In many cases, this would involve taking a trip with the child. If the clinic makes provision for the testing of hearing in young children, for interviews and some guidance of the parents, and offers assistance in the training of the young deaf child, such a trip is worth while. Parents are advised against taking frequent long trips with very young children, especially if each trip means a series of "tests." But if financial and geographical conditions permit, and if arrangements may be made with the clinic, then monthly visits, or even three or four visits a year, can help both the parent and the child.[222]

Many towns and cities, and some villages and rural areas, which make no provision for the education of the young deaf child, do provide nursery school education for hearing children and parents' classes in child development. There are also parent-teacher associations and psychology classes for parents in some areas. The parent of the deaf child should take advantage of such opportunities if it is possible. Such participation offers the parent a chance to educate the community in some degree about the deaf child; to observe hearing children; to obtain guidance for herself which should assist her in understanding the importance of parent-child relationships and in guiding her child as a child.

Where no such facilities exist, and if the parents are planning to visit a clinic, a school for the deaf, or any other center for guidance, they would be well-advised to investigate by correspondence—with the university, the board of education, the health and welfare agencies, or the League for the Hard-of-Hearing in that city they plan to visit—the possible opportunities for them to visit nursery schools for hearing children or for deaf children or for both, and for them to observe any work with children of preschool age, either deaf or hearing, and work with parents. If both parents go, or one parent and another adult, the trip will be more valuable, since one of the adults can take care of the child while the other visits and observes.

There are situations where the parents find it quite impossible to travel to another town and must be entirely dependent for some time upon help through correspondence. In such instances, it is important that *both* parents get all they possibly can through correspondence with as many authentic agencies as they can reach. It is important for every deaf child to have both mother *and father* participating actively in every phase of his development, but it is a *must* if the parents are entirely dependent upon correspondence for help. Reading of pamphlets, journals, and books on child development, parent guidance, the education of the deaf, etc., with follow-up discussions by the parents are essential.

A wise choice of reading material will save the parent time and confusion. Competent persons in a center to which the parent may write will gladly advise what to read.[135, 166]

Parent, Teacher, Child

Some parents have at their disposal teachers, preschool or nursery school classes for deaf children, or a speech and hearing clinic. It is only normal that these parents, like all other parents of deaf children, want the "best" for their respective children. Their attitudes may change after the deafness is discovered, but in spite of the feelings of hopelessness, rejection, over-protection, or withdrawal which may have been aroused in them, the parents continue to want the "best." The fact of deafness baffles them and they seek help. Some parents want to secure a teacher immediately, who will teach the child and assume the whole burden of orientating him to his world. An increasing number of parents, wishing to assume some of the responsibility themselves, are at a loss how to begin.

The teacher or the clinician, to whom the parent goes, is in the fortunate position of being able to discuss with the parent the importance of the parents' participation in the child's total development, including the development of language and speech.

In the initial stages, the teacher, since she is more familiar with the problems of deafness, has a better understanding of the aims and responsibilities, and she must therefore impress upon the parents that she cannot solve the problem alone, and that she will do her job better if she has the full cooperation of both parents.

In a sense, teacher and parent want the same for the child—emotional stability, social development, intellectual achievement, good health, and the acquisition of skills that include under standing of language and speech.[7] The teacher's viewpoints, how ever, cannot be the same as the parents' and she dare not try to assume the role that rightly belongs to the parents.[86] Their emotional drive is different from hers, but each has a definite contribution to make. Each must recognize her specific role while, at the same time, both make every effort to cooperate and make the child's life a happy, integrated whole.[87] These principles should be kept in mind and practiced whether there is access to a nursery school, a parent education class, a correspondence course, a clinic, a tutor, or any combination of such services.[65]

The Feeling of Adequacy

The task of educating as many people as possible to their various roles in meeting the problems of deafness in early childhood could not be described as "easy," and is often a long, slow process. The ease and speed with which it is carried out depend chiefly on the personality of the person taking the lead, and next on the persons who must be trained to become leaders in some capacity. Most of the people who should be given information and guidance are able to understand "the words." But to bring them to a state of feeling adequate in their roles, so that they can and dare to act on their own initiative, is probably the most important and most difficult part of the task.

There is the family friend who doesn't feel "comfortable" talking to a child who can't hear. There is the parent who wants to do everything possible for her child, but feels that the teacher can do a better job alone. There is the teacher who can accept intellectually the importance of parent participation but who becomes nervous, compulsive, authoritative, over-enthusiastic, too "sweet," or too behavior-conscious in the actual situation.

The family friend can be given time to adjust to the child, to watch improvements as someone else does the guiding. The teacher can be transferred to another position for which she is better suited, and replaced by a steadier teacher. But *the parent remains,* adequate or not, and *the child remains.*[81]

Steps must be taken from the first moment of the interview, and throughout the parent-teacher relationship, to make the parent feel adequate. This can't be done merely by telling the parent that she *is* adequate. It means giving out information as fast as the individual parent can assimilate it, showing the parent what she can do and how to do it, accepting the parent's "mistakes," suggestions, and even criticisms, and giving her support, at the same time that everything possible is being done to make her independent of that support.[189]

The teacher who is generally considered the source of education will do all she can do to strengthen the relationship between parent and child, by guidance of each, by giving psychological help when necessary and possible; she will not hold back information nor impose points of view that could limit parent and child.[6]

The Young Child Needs His Home

Nothing can replace a happy home in the life of the young child. For that reason, he should be kept at home, and educated in the home and by local facilities where they exist, for as long as possible.

There are situations where, in spite of the availability of excellent help, the parent absolutely refuses to recognize her role, to accept help, to assume the usual responsibility of any parent for any child, and who, in spite of knowing that she could help the child and help the teacher make her work more effective, will not cooperate. There may be situations where the child is "dragged" to a teacher once a week, carrying with him all the distressed feelings and the problems resulting from the unhappiness in his home; where any benefit from the training ceases the moment he leaves the teacher—and there the matter rests. What happens to that child over a period of time is an indescribably sad story.[130] Deaf children of preschool age who are enmeshed in these or similar circumstances would be far happier in another home or in a good residential school.

There are excellent residential schools in this country where emphasis is placed on oral communication and the individual child, and where the interest of the parent who must be separated from the child is invited and encouraged.

The existence of good residential schools, however, should not be made the reason for sending the very young deaf child away from home. For, no matter how good a school may be, it cannot give to the little child what a good home can give.[164]

Let it be repeated: Everyone has a role to play. Parents, teachers, children, and community are included in the educational process, and cooperation among the various elements is necessary. Attention must be given to fundamentals of the educational training of the child, to a more specific discussion of the special aspects of the education of the young deaf child, and to background information which will make the teacher's and the parent's guidance of the child more effective.

PART 1

Fundamentals of the Training

CHAPTER 1

Language

The language element must be given priority over any other in the training of the deaf child, especially the *young* deaf child. Each parent and each specialist has his own ideas concerning the deaf child's needs. The ideas may center upon speech, auditory training, hearing aids, lipreading, intelligence tests, reading, writing, psychological guidance for the parents, play therapy for the child, or upon nursery school activities, and each of these centers is important as a part of the total picture. However, it must be forcefully emphasized that no method can be effective nor any objective attained, unless it is viewed, understood, and employed in relation to *language*.

Language is not only the *objective* in mind for the deaf child; it is also the *means*. Creative activities and free play as means of expression are language experiences. Lipreading is merely a tool for the understanding of spoken language in relation to situations, people, and things. Sense training as a means of expression, and of developing the ability to concentrate, observe, and think, is a language experience. Auditory training is a tool for the development of better voice quality, a broader concept of spoken language, and a consciousness of language in the environment. Proficiency in reading is based on language experiences, and reading itself is a language experience. Speech or articulated language is dependent upon an understanding of spoken language in relation to other language experiences.

The child's thoughts as they are expressed in many ways are a form of language.[171] His feelings, as they are expressed in various ways—as a cry, in laughter, in negative reactions or cooperative attitudes, and, later on, through speech—are a form of language. His relationships with his parents, with children, with his teacher, and with other individuals, are each expressed in some way, and whether or not the avenues of expression are obvious or not, they constitute a language which may "speak" more forcefully than any words could. The language of feelings is very important and must not be overlooked while striving to cope with any other form of language necessary to the deaf child's development.[173]

It would be a great error to restrict our concept of the term "language" to the spoken form or to the printed form. Understanding of the spoken word and, much later, of the printed word, is essential to the deaf child, and steps must be taken from the earliest possible moment to reach such understanding. The attainment of the objective, however, is dependent upon a recognition of all other phases of the child's development as furnishing powerful tributaries in the total language system.[184]

The speech teacher must be a language teacher; the lipreading teacher is a language teacher; the teacher of reading is a teacher of language; the nursery school teacher is a language teacher; the parent who guides and cares for her child constantly is a teacher of language.

Language and every aspect of the child's development are inter-related; and any particular area of that development, which may not be itself a language, will be related to language in some respect and will contribute to language.

In the pages that follow, it has been necessary to divide the total language training into parts, and to divide those parts into smaller sections, in order to clarify facts and ideas for a broader understanding and for more effective use. The worker, however, whether parent or teacher, is cautioned against losing sight of the *whole* while studying or using the *part*.

Principles to Work By

In guiding the young deaf child, in the home, in the nursery school, or in the play yard, two principles must be adhered to by parent and teacher: (1) His needs *as a child* must be provided for, by exposure to a normal, happy environment in which he may enjoy the activities and experiences of the hearing child.[8, 115] (2) His needs *as a deaf child* must be met, by special, consciously designed methods employed by the adults who guide him.

In practice, the parent and the teacher make every effort to combine both principles in such a way that the "special" skills which the child must acquire will blend into his everyday experiences. The person who is familiar with the problems of deafness and with the principles of child development realizes that failure to attend to both areas results in a limited and limiting training. It is quite possible to combine developmental growth and the special training, and the latter is more effective if it is made an outgrowth of the former.

These principles will be kept in mind as the *whole* language factor is divided, discussed, and read about under such headings as those that follow in this section. When the worker is concerned with speech, she considers not only the speech exercise, but also how the idea may be combined with lipreading, auditory training, sense training, developmental activities, and with the child's experiences and interests, to facilitate and accelerate language development.

CHAPTER 2

Lipreading or Speech Reading—Language

It has been mentioned that the eyes of the deaf child have to take over many of the jobs that the eyes and ears of the hearing child assume. In time, the hearing child is able to interpret what is being said through hearing alone, without having to watch the speaker, and he also develops an ability to interpret, through hearing, many things being *done* although the actions, within earshot, may be out of his line of vision. The deaf child is never in this fortunate position. He must use his eyes and other senses he possesses in a normal capacity to make up for the lack of hearing.

He has to use his eyes in learning to understand spoken language. This operation is referred to as *lipreading* or *speech reading*. In the discussion of methods it is described as the *visual* method.

Lipreading, although its obvious meaning would appear to be the reading of the lips, implies considerably more than that. Since the little deaf child must be given an early and "right" start in lipreading for the development of language understanding, the demands of lipreading and the difficulties involved should be made clear to those who are guiding the child.[57]

SOME DIFFICULTIES AND DEMANDS

Two hearing adults have only to try lipreading each other's natural speech as each stands on either side of a glass door, or by watching a silent movie with no captions, to get some conception of the difficulties involved in interpreting spoken language through lipreading. It becomes all too evident that spoken language has been developed as a means of communication between persons who hear.[82]

Every hearing person, especially those who work with deaf children or who plan to do so, should try to place himself or herself in the position of *having* to lipread, for a better understanding of the child's problem. The person will find himself, no doubt, straining either to catch a thread of sound or squinting to see more, in the urge to tear down the barrier between himself and the speaker; or looking around frantically at the same time he is trying to watch the continuous speech of the speaker, in an attempt to get some clue as to what is being said.

Many a person who has subjected himself to such a situation, and who has tried with all his might to understand, sinks with relief into the nearest chair and groans, "It's AWFUL!" This is a normal reaction by people with a wealth of language experiences behind them.

The most "awful" part of the situation is that people tend to go through life taking language and its by-product, speech, too much for granted, whether one has hearing or no hearing. Factors which make understanding of speech a difficult task on occasion for the hearing person combine into an enormous problem for the person who doesn't hear.

Grammatical forms, rapid speech, very slow speech, slurred pronunciation, and facial expression or lack of it, on the part of the speaker, all affect the lipreader. It is the duty of every person to know *how* to talk. However, since many hearing people continue to think in terms of *what* they say rather than *how,* the deaf child must develop many qualities which will make lipreading of the majority more possible. He must develop quickness and alertness of mind, concentration, visual memory, subconscious grasp of meaning, and intuition, to supplement the speech which he is able to see and interpret.

Such abilities cannot be developed if training the young deaf child to lipread is restricted to the reading of the lips alone. Exercise in speech reading must be made a part of his life from day to day.

LIPREADING TAKES TIME

This lipreading skill, which is necessary to the child's understanding of language in all respects and which must come before speech, must be developed as early in life as possible. In spite of its many real demands on the child, it can be developed while he is still at the preschool level in the course of daily living, depending on how it is done, and on the attitude of the person who is leading the way.

There must be neither hurry nor impatience, and there must be no discouragement if the child does not learn to lipread quickly. He will establish either positive or negative attitudes towards lipreading according to whether it is presented to him enjoyably or as a painful chore.

The first requirement in training the child to lipread is that everyone *talk* to him whenever it is possible and plausible to do so. The act of talking however is not sufficient. The parent and the teacher must talk about something related to the child in the situation where he is found, to something which the child can see, either as an object or an action.[185]

If he is exposed to speech in a happy environment, if everyone talks to him in real situations, and if he is encouraged, not forced, to watch the faces of speakers, he will begin to connect the movements of the speaker's lips and face with the object, the person, or the action of the moment. This recognition does not come swiftly. There are seldom immediate results in lipreading. The child must see the words spoken in the same relationship many times, just as the hearing child has to hear them many times, before understanding comes. It does come, however, to a gratifying and often surprising degree, if both parent and teacher will be content to give the child the experiences and the time he requires.[183]

THE PARENTS' CONCERNS

Many parents, especially those who have been working with their children for a short time only, regard it as a problem that their respective children are often unwilling to watch their (the parents') faces. Far too much concern is aroused by this unwillingness.

Suppose the adult starts to train the child to lipread the word *ball*. She holds the colored object in her hand and talks to the child about it. "This is a ball, Billy. It's a pretty ball." What does the child see? He sees a mouth moving, or something happening to the whole face, but he also sees the ball, and that is more interesting to him.

He probably wants to hold it, to make it a part of himself, and to know more about this wonderful, bright thing before him. This is not only a normal reaction but a highly constructive one. After the child has had more experience with the ball and has derived some personal satisfaction from that experience, he will be more willing to look at the speaker's face. To some extent he realizes that the movements of the mouth and face relate to the plaything, and realizes more and more that everything that concerns him is related to those peculiar movements.

At first, the lip movements are merely a part of the whole expression in the whole situation. If the whole is attractive enough, and *if there is no compulsion to respond,* the child will begin to notice details. He will observe differences as well as similarities, and will notice that certain lip and facial movements go with one object or situation, while other movements go with another object or situation.

Many a parent has felt that the child pays too little attention to the lips, and too much attention to the whole face. This is only normal, as the whole means more to any young child than the part. Furthermore, the child's attention to the whole expression is essential to proficient lipreading.

In consideration of the child's tendency to notice the whole, with himself as the center, the teacher and the parent must know that a tense, harsh, anxious approach will cause him to withdraw before he realizes what the lip movements can mean to him.

It can not be repeated too often that the parent or the teacher who is starting lipreading with the young deaf child must be content to "pour out" speech without asking the child to indicate at once that he understands. Some children take twice or three times as long as other children take to indicate understanding through lipreading. This apparent "slowness" in lipreading is not necessarily a sign of retardation, of inability to learn to lipread, nor of any other negative sign. The indication will come in time, but it must come spontaneously if the child is to enjoy the process of learning to read the lips, and eventually to become a good lipreader.[210]

Once it is clearly understood that language understanding through lipreading is essential to speech development, the parents' anxiety for speech, which still prevails, sometimes leads to forceful methods in lipreading situations. A parent may have been told, and rightly so, that she should not attempt any formal "teaching" of speech, but that she may prepare for speech through starting lipreading with the child. Unless she is given further guidance in the lipreading process, all her drives and resources may be so concentrated in the lipreading training that she forgets the child, and does more breaking down than preparing.

One parent began to train her eighteen-month-old deaf child through the John Tracy Clinic Correspondence Course. She became disturbed almost immediately because he would not sit still and watch her as she talked. She was advised against attempting to "make" him sit still and watch her. A hearing child would not do this under the happiest of conditions; why should the deaf child? She was further advised to attempt no formal lip-reading work at this time, but to use every opportunity to talk to him casually, to sing, to play with him, and to enjoy him.

When he was twenty-three months old, his mother brought him to the Clinic to get an opinion from the teacher concerning his progress. He lipread simple words and directions for his mother and for the teacher, and no gestures were used by either adult. It was apparent too that the relationship between mother and child was a comfortable one.

The mother was asked how she had accomplished such results in lipreading. Her reply was that she didn't know exactly when the lipreading began, but that the child seemed to begin understanding what his mother and father said a short time after they stopped trying to "make" him read their lips.

Another parent, who had not started training until the child was four years of age, reported a somewhat similar experience with her child and made the following very cogent remark, "I suppose he figured that if *I* wanted to work so hard doing *his* job there wasn't much point in his doing it!"

GENERAL AND SPECIFIC ASPECTS

Lipreading may be divided into two categories, (1) *general* lipreading and (2) *specific* lipreading.

General lipreading is the term applied to the comprehension of spontaneous and natural language encountered by the child during the day, in those situations which tend to be common to all children, and in which no effort is made to "teach" specific words, phrases, or other language forms. It is concerned mainly with general meanings, concepts, and understandings.

Specific lipreading is the term applied to the comprehension of specific words, to the conscious building of a lipreading vocabulary, and tends to take place in the "lesson" or deliberately contrived situation.

Specific lipreading tends to be an outgrowth of general lipreading. Both terms should be understood by the worker to enable her to give attention to all areas of lipreading and to keep closer check on the child's progress. Specific and general lipreading overlap in practice almost constantly.

In both cases, the parent and the teacher talk to the child in simple language suitable to his age and related to a familiar experience. Lighting should be good to avoid eyestrain and tension. The speaker uses normal conversational speech without mouthing, facial contortions, or exaggerations. Children have a tendency to exaggerate anyway, and if they are exposed constantly to exaggerated speech, they will learn to use speech of that nature, and may even exaggerate the exaggerated.

A discussion of each of these categories should give the parent and the teacher further assistance in organizing the child's program and in answering the question, "How do I know if he is getting all that he should be getting?"

CHAPTER 3

General Lipreading—Language

There are almost as many opportunities for general lipreading as there are incidents in the daily life of the child. Even before the child goes to nursery school, if that becomes a possibility for him, the parents talk to him and play with him just as the parents of any hearing child would do.[3] It doesn't matter if the child shows little or no understanding of what is being "said." The parents talk to him anyway. The hearing infant and young child do not "understand" all the things a mother says to either of them as each is being bathed, dressed, cuddled, etc., but this does not cause the mother to cease talking, laughing, and singing when she is with her child. Just as the hearing baby in time begins to recognize a connection between such performances, between things being *done* and things being *said,* so does the deaf child, although the ability of the deaf child to interpret specific *words* may take much longer.

Lipreading is not only an experience in itself, it is a part of every experience of the child.

"LIPREADING IDEAS" IS IMPORTANT

Real conversation is essential to the child's language growth. Expressions such as "Come to lunch," "It's time to go to bed," "Let's go to the store," "Where are your shoes?" "Get your coat," "Here's Daddy," and others, are a natural part of the daily life of any child, and the parent and the teacher should grasp every opportunity to expose the little deaf child to the same expressions.

The deaf child learns to connect the lip and facial movements with events *that concern him* and which are therefore more meaningful to him. When he sees his mother working around the kitchen, setting the table, and finally saying to him, "Come to dinner," he is not only learning to understand the expression from reading the lips but also from making use of clues, such as his mother's activity, the food on the table, etc. His concept of the "words" is broadened through his understanding of the situation related to the words.

In such instances, the mother may say that Jimmy really isn't lipreading, that he is merely getting the idea from the situation. *It is extremely important that he does learn to get the idea from the situation.* That is actually the child's first indication of lipreading, and is as essential to language understanding and proficient lipreading as the comprehension of the isolated word.

Complete sentences uttered in connection with a given situation are as easily understood by the young deaf child as are single words, and if he sees them often enough in the same relationship, he eventually learns to lipread them "objectively." That is, he understands the phrases and sentences more and more independently of visible clues, such as the table, the food, etc., as in the above example.

The ability to get the general concept of a sentence, to "lipread ideas," is one of the fundamental requirements of language development. For this reason, the parent must be cautioned against restricting her training of the child to "lessons" or "drills" on isolated words. If a choice between general lipreading and specific lipreading had to be made by a parent, the wise choice would be general lipreading.

TALK: DON'T GESTURE

There is often a temptation to gesture to a deaf child, even while talking to him, especially if he does not understand immediately. For instance, while saying, "Go and get your coat; we're going out," it may seem easy to make the gesture of putting on a coat. Unfortunately, the child will pay more attention to the gesture than to the speaker's face. This is natural for him since he tends to be impressed by the "bigness" of things, and the movements of the arms and the body are "bigger" and more noticeable than the movements of the mouth.[220]

If the child doesn't understand, the adult should go and find the coat, show it to the child, and talk about it— "This is your coat. Put it on. We're going out." In time, the child is able to understand the sentence without such assistance from the adult and without depending on the unnatural gesture. Constant exposure to such "gesturing experiences" could breed a dependence on gestures and could limit his growth in many respects.

No one with a knowledge of lipreading or of his own language would say merely "bed" if the occasion calls for using the word in a sentence. Furthermore, there are all kinds of beds in many different situations and all must be learned at some time by the deaf child; for example, "It's time to go to bed," or "Let's go to bed," or "The baby has gone to bed," or "Put the dolly to bed," or "Mother is going to make the bed," etc.

After the child has been exposed to the word *bed* in many different associations, he not only learns to lipread the word more easily in the specific lipreading situation, but also he understands that *bed* may be associated with a number of situations and people. The young child loves repetition (not drills) and through pleasurable repetition every object or action that is a part of his daily experience becomes associated, in his thinking and his understanding, with other words. And so he is learning about *language*.[119]

35

USE "LANGUAGE THAT LIVES"

In the case of the child who is in nursery school, casual and enthusiastic talks between teacher and child, or parent and child (even though the adult does most of the talking), provide the earliest opportunities for tying up home and school activities.[178] Home and school should harmonize as much as possible, to make the child's life an integrated whole.[141]

The teacher would have snapshots of the child's home and his family, and the parent would have pictures at home of nursery school life. As the teacher and the parent talk to the child about things that happened at home, at school, or downtown, he is taking his first steps towards an understanding of the language relating to time and distance, abstractions which could present difficulties in later years if he has not been prepared for them.[35]

No attempt is made to "teach" the tenses of the verb, nor to make the child indicate an awareness of the use of certain phrases or other language forms; but the adult uses them naturally and casually just as she would in talking to the child who hears.

No good will come of creating a special language for the little deaf child. It is not easier for him. If a word such as *yesterday* or *again* would be used in a particular situation in talking to any child, the adult would use it in talking to the deaf child. Omitting it will not simplify understanding for the child, and may make the adult's speech and manner stilted and unnatural. The use of it does not necessarily entail an explanation of its meaning as a separate entity. The whole idea expressed in the sentence is what the child is interested in, and is what he must learn to understand.

Of course, there comes the time when the deaf child has become so conscious of spoken language, not only in terms of whole concepts, but of parts of sentences, that he will ask what something means. This may happen early or late depending on the individual child.[197] Although this is a highly acceptable development, it is often disconcerting for the parent and even the teacher who may feel "put on the spot," suddenly realizing the complications of our language, and the difficulties involved in "explaining" a word or expression which we use glibly day after day.

There are many single words which cannot be illustrated through pictures, and the adult is forced to use *situations* and *descriptive sentences* to *show* the child what is meant.

Take for example the case of the severely deaf five-year-old who was in her third year in nursery school, and whose parents had participated in her training from the time her deafness was discovered. During a play-house situation she was washing dishes used at a tea party. She began to take clean dishes and wash them after clearing away the ones that had been used. The teacher said, "That's not necessary, Beth. You don't have to wash the clean dishes."

Beth agreed; but, to the teacher's surprise, she responded with, " 'That's not necessary.' What's that?" The speech would not have been intelligible to a person who had not followed the events and conversation to that point. However, in the circumstances, it was understood by the teacher.

The teacher had to use as many objects and actions to which the expression might be applied as the facilities at hand would permit. And she used the expression in each instance. What she was able to do at that time did not cover every situation in which such an expression would be used, but it served for the time being to satisfy Beth's curiosity and to add to her understanding.

The explanation, limited as it had to be at the time, produced some interesting results. A few days later, Beth's mother asked the teacher if she had any idea where Beth might have learned to use an expression that sounded like, "That's not necessary." The teacher related the events of the previous situation.

37

The mother said that when she began washing some china that had not been in use for a while and which she intended using for some guests, Beth quickly informed her mother, "That's not necessary. Not dirty." The mother took the time to explain to Beth and to show her how dust collected, etc., so that in this case the dishes had to be washed.

Most five-year-old deaf children in all probability would not use the above expression, but they do adopt other expressions which are used casually in their respective environments. But they will not learn to use them if the adults try to establish a "special" language for them.

Every parent and every teacher, at some time, will encounter situations where they have to explain to the child. Since most such explanations have to be made by getting across the whole idea, it is important that from the first the child be exposed to "language that lives." Imagine the predicament of the adult if she attempted to explain each word in the expression, "That's not necessary"!

Parents and teachers give the child the language of society, make him feel understood when he tries to use that language, and give him explanations as concrete and as comprehensive as possible in the given circumstances.[217]

The basis of general lipreading might well be: Concept first, the whole before the part.

CHAPTER 4

Specific Lipreading—Language

The deaf child needs words. He must learn to use them in speaking, but before he reaches that stage, he must learn to understand them through lipreading. General lipreading experiences provide him with a familiarity with many words, and out of these experiences the parent and the teacher make a conscious effort to build a lipreading vocabulary. The so-called lipreading "lesson" has been designed for this purpose.

It has been stated that the child first appears to understand through physical clues. Then he gets a general concept of spoken language through a combination of what he sees on the lips with the physical clues which the situation provides. These stages are important since they develop naturally out of the child's everyday life.

There is a need, however, to go beyond this point. The child must learn to recognize verbal clues as well as physical ones. The verbal clue may be a particular word in the whole sentence, one which he lipreads easily and which helps to make his interpretation and response faster and more accurate.

Because of the characteristics of the language, the child is certain to miss or misinterpret some words in sentences, in spite of all the vocabulary building that may be done. Not all spoken language is visible to the lipreader, so that he must always be somewhat dependent on physical clues. However, the more words he can recognize, the fewer he will miss or misinterpret, and the less dependent he will be upon physical clues.

Guided by the parent and the teacher in understanding words related to specific objects or actions, the child learns to lipread exact words spoken. If he is given enough of the "right kind" of practice, he may develop an impressive ability to point out pictures or objects, or perform actions at command.

It must be remembered, however, that an impressive list of words is quite useless in the total educational accomplishment unless the child understands their relation to other words and to his everyday life. For example, a young deaf child may be able to give an outstanding performance in lipreading in the school-room, but, once away from that environment, none of the words may mean anything to him.

Specific lipreading training will be effective only to the degree that it is made an outgrowth of general lipreading and the accompanying real experiences are related to casual spoken language. This does not imply that general lipreading stops when the specific is begun, nor that specific lipreading must be delayed until a defined period of time has been devoted to general lip-reading. It does imply, however, that the rate at which the child can assimilate and understand isolated words will depend on the extent to which he has been exposed to spoken language in the home. Also, the choice of words for specific lipreading will derive in some degree from the child's past experiences and from his preferences for certain objects, activities, etc., which have been observed earlier.

Parents and teachers are constantly advised against regarding the vocabulary acquired by a certain child at a certain age as the norm in guiding other children of that age in specific lipreading. Differences in home environment, individual interests, and differences in personality will have some effect on the content and extent of each vocabulary.[44]

Some children learn to lipread and understand number con

cepts earlier than other children. Some find colors easy to understand, while others who may be able to match colors easily take
twice or three times as long to learn to lipread the names of
colors. A child's attitude towards colors or numbers or actions
could have some bearing on the time required for him to learn
to lipread them.

Such considerations must influence our guidance of the young
deaf child in the building of a lipreading vocabulary.

THE "RIGHT" WORDS

The person who is to guide the child may ask, "Where shall
I start? What are the right words?" One has only to watch the
child in the midst of various situations—with toys, with puzzles,
with pictures, with other children, with his parents and other
adults—to get some idea of his preferences and so establish a
starting point for specific lipreading.

Of course, one might say that all children like to play, that
all children like toys, and that all children must learn this word
or that word. Although it is unwise to be over-cautious, it is also
unwise to make sweeping generalizations under which one might
minimize the importance of the child's individuality.

The adult must consider what the child appears to enjoy most,
to enjoy least, to be frustrated by, to be challenged by, to give
most attention to. One might say that such investigations could
go on for months, and delay the necessary training. They not
only could go on, they should go on. This should not, however,
cause any serious delay in beginning specific lipreading.

Everyone at some time or other has heard the parent of a
hearing child remark that Billy is "just crazy" about cars, airplanes, and all kinds of machinery. In all probability, that parent
didn't have to sit and take notes on her child every day of his
three years to discover this interest. She accepted his interest,
encouraged it, and continued to expose him to other activities
and objects. A special interest does not indicate that the people

41

in the child's environment must cease talking about other objects and activities, nor that the child will fail to acquire other interests and the corresponding words. The interest, however, should be used as a starting point.

The parent who has been *with* her child all the way should not have any difficulty in knowing *what words* to use in beginning specific lipreading. The teacher who has been trained in the observation of children as well as in the special requirements of the young deaf child, will discover in a relatively short time *where* to start.

If cars and airplanes seem to be the chief interest, *car* and *airplane* would be chosen for the first lipreading lesson. They may be in the form of toys, form boards, or, if the child is older, in pictured form also. Several toy cars and toy airplanes might be used. Each time the adult holds up a car, points to it, or gives it to the child, she talks about it in a pleasant way, permitting child and object to remain the center of interest while spoken language is used.

Generally speaking, to make use of the familiar and interesting object saves time in getting the "lesson" under way. If a disliked object is used, the child may react negatively or lose interest quickly—more quickly than his age-level would indicate. If an *unfamiliar* attractive object is used, the adult may have more than an "average" difficulty in getting the child's attention. He will want to play and experiment with the toy. This desire should be fulfilled.

Once this "new" object has become a familiar part of the child's life, he is more apt to cooperate in the lipreading situation. Probably he still likes the object, already knows a lot about it, and what the teacher or parent is doing with it now will tell him more about it. His previous satisfactions and his ever-present curiosity promote cooperation.[46]

In the first lipreading lessons, only two or three objects are used at one time. Much repetition of each word is required. How-

42

ever, the same objects should not be used day after day, week after week. If possible, the teacher and the parent would use many different kinds of toy cars, varying in size and color, and would improvise activities with the cars, to maintain interest while the child is being given the necessary repetition in lipreading *car*. If he begins to lose interest in a particular toy, it may be put aside for a few days and brought back later. Usually the child accepts it with renewed interest.[195]

TALK IN SENTENCES

Although certain words are made the core of the specific lipreading period, single words do not make good lipreading material. Each word should be presented in sentences so the child may get an early start in making the necessary associations between two words or more.

"This is a *ball*, Jimmy. It's a *big ball*. It rolls. See, the *ball* rolls like this. Now, you have the *ball*, Jimmy. Roll the *ball* to me. Oh, you rolled the *ball!*"

The whole word in the whole sentence not only puts across the word, but prepares the child for lipreading of specific phrases such as *a big ball, a red ball,* etc. In the process of teaching lipreading, specific or general, teacher and parent are concerned with the development of meaningful language for broadening thought and for understanding ideas.

LANGUAGE FORMS

Specific lipreading periods must include exercises that will help to establish as many of the language forms common and necessary to every child as the little deaf child is able to absorb.

The teacher and the parent cannot continue to "teach" only nouns. Verbs, adjectives, and other parts of speech must be given attention.

They would be presented, specifically, to the deaf child in an order paralleling that in which they are learned by the hearing

43

child. Children are interested in objects; therefore, nouns tend to be the first language form presented. Action verbs might be presented about the same time. Part of the "lesson" might be devoted to nouns, part to action verbs, and in some cases to a combination.

It is not uncommon to find that some deaf children learn to lipread action verbs such as *jump, run, walk,* etc., before learning to lipread as many nouns.[2]

Adjectives, including color, number, and contrasting adjectives such as *big* and *small, hot* and *cold,* follow nouns and action verbs, and sometimes overlap.

A few minutes of each day would be devoted to the establishment of such language forms, according to the child's attention span, his interests, his readiness. All lessons would be short, interesting, and a form of play. Whenever possible, specific lipreading would be combined with speech preparation and auditory training. Every lesson should be supplemented in other situations, in and out of school and home, by exposure to general lipreading situations, so that lipreading goes on throughout each day.

THE "DIFFICULT" CHILD

In any group of families where there are deaf children, and in almost any nursery school for deaf children, there will be a child, or some children, who need special attention, and who may be referred to as "difficult." [64] Not infrequently, the specific lesson situation supplies the spark that starts the fire.

If many restrictions have been placed on the deaf child from a very early age, whether those restrictions have centered upon his behavior, eating, toilet training, or some matter related to the deafness; and if, at the age of three, four, or five, the child finds himself in a permissive atmosphere for the first time in his life; it is only natural that he try to make up for all the fun he has missed and seize upon outlets for expression of which he has been wrongfully deprived.[9]

His actions may be so extreme, so negative, so aggressive, so "abnormal," that neither he nor the adult makes any progress in a lesson.[1] The causes of such exceptional behavior must be found and removed, but both teacher and parent must realize that pressure on the child will not solve the problem in any sense.[51]

Whenever possible, the parents of that child must be reached and helped, and the child must be given more freedom, more respect as an individual, and more understanding.[19]

TRAVEL AT THE CHILD'S RATE

The little deaf child, in specific lipreading as in any other learning situation, can travel only at his own rate, and he should be encouraged and stimulated to develop at full capacity. If the situations at home and at school are enjoyable, he will feel that his effort is worth while in itself, and he will develop a persistence, through pleasant experiences related to lipreading which will drive through to success.[28]

CHAPTER 5

Speech–Language

Just as speech in the hearing person has been taken for granted, so has the lack of it in the deaf person been taken for granted by many people. A child is born, he is cared for, he eats, he sleeps, laughs, cries, and eventually walks and talks. The earlier he talks the prouder are his parents and the more admiring are their friends and neighbors. In spite of the premium that is placed on the child's ability to talk at an early age, few persons give thought to what is involved in the development of that highly prized tool for intercourse.

Speech does not appear miraculously from nowhere for no reason, in any person, and an understanding of its development in the young deaf child demands some understanding of its development in the hearing child.

THE HEARING CHILD–THE DEAF CHILD

Normal speech development in the hearing child follows approximately one general order: (1) birth cry, (2) cries that express needs and desires, (3) laughing, (4) babbling (vowel sounds first), (5) understanding of spoken language, (6) imitation of speech, (7) invented words, (8) speech to achieve something, (9) one-word sentences—nouns and verbs first; prepositions, pronouns, conjunctions, etc., much later, (10) sentences and phrases in haphazard order, (11) correct sentences.[185]

The hearing child progresses from stage to stage as he hears spoken language day after day, and eventually he gives back what he hears in the manner and in the situations in which he heard it. The deaf child goes through the first stages of laughing, crying, and babbling in a relatively normal way. Like the hearing baby, he enjoys the bodily sensations which occur in laughing and babbling. However, he cannot go on to the next stage, understanding of spoken language, unless special efforts are made to render him aware of speech through some medium other than hearing.

UNDERSTANDING BEFORE SPEECH

Speech develops through the understanding of language—not only an understanding of articulated language (speech), but also through an understanding of the language of feelings, thought, and experience.[172]

The hearing child *hears* speech consciously and unconsciously from the day he is born. He hears speech in relation to everything about him—to the feelings of his parents, to their actions, and to many experiences directly and indirectly associated with his life. And just as he gives back the love, the hate, the resentment, the frustration, the security, the happiness, or the anxieties, which he has absorbed from his environment, he also gives back the speech to which he has been exposed.[16]

The deaf child absorbs all the influences that have to do with feelings and experiences except the influence of speech; and he reflects these influences in his behavior but not through speech. He must be trained to understand speech in order that he may use it. His feelings, attitudes, interests, and experiences must not be impoverished or limited by depriving him of this training.

The parent of the young deaf child—as, later on, the teacher—begins to make optimum use of the normal senses of sight, touch, smell, and taste. And special auditory training is begun also, to develop any residual hearing which the child may have. Parent and teacher must employ methods designed to develop a speech that is as normal as possible; hence, the pattern of speech development in the hearing child is followed as closely as possible.

The hearing child is exposed to speech that has meaning—not to isolated vowels and consonants, but to whole words, phrases, and sentences that express ideas.[145] The same principle must be applied in the training of the young deaf child. Adherence to this principle will result not only in the child's developing a broad understanding of spoken language, but in his wanting to talk and in his having something to talk about. This understanding of verbalized ideas and words, which must come before speech, grows out of the general and specific lipreading which has been discussed.

People talk to the child about everything that is a part of his daily life. He learns to watch speakers, and to realize that he can do with his mouth what they do with theirs. He learns that, when he uses his voice in a certain way, he gets a more satisfying and prompt response.

As the child becomes more aware of speech and its meaning for him, he begins to imitate and to go through many of the stages of speech development that the hearing child experiences.

A GENERAL APPROACH

The child's use of his voice, in babbling and in imitating, must be encouraged. Every time the child babbles, chatters, or tries to imitate, even though the utterance is unintelligible, the adult should respond orally and accept the child's attempts at communication. This might be called a general approach to speech, an approach in which everyone may participate.

The deaf baby may wave his fist in a vague, general direction and say, "Ba!" The parent would not ignore this. The increased volume of his voice and his persistence in saying "Ba" may indicate that the baby wants something which he is as yet unable to go and get.

The mother responds with, "Ba? You want Ba? What's Ba?" The baby may continue in a demanding tone of voice, "Bababa!" The mother proceeds to find out what the baby wants, and talks about it. "Do you want the block?" and holds up a block. The baby may yell louder than ever, "Ba! Ba! Ba!" The mother looks around, sees a ball, holds it up, and says, "Do you want the ball?"

The baby may stretch out his arms eagerly and excitedly say, "Bababa," indicating that his desire has at last been fulfilled.

Incidents like this provide a simple, natural source for language understanding through lipreading and for speech development. Speech in similar situations can be especially effective when it is made a part of a response to a need.[40]

The adult's sincere attempts to understand the young deaf child when he wants something, wants to do something, or is seeking for an explanation, are of great importance in the general speech preparation. The child's spontaneous "remarks," during play or his participation in creative and other developmental activities, receive attention whether they are intelligible, partly intelligible, or unintelligible. The adult gives the child the correct words and spoken language, but the child's attempts at imitation should be accepted without the situation being turned into a painful, formal, corrective speech "lesson." [23]

For example, if a three-year-old deaf child comes to his mother with an "I want" look on his face and says, "Uppa," the mother quickly tries to understand what he wants. It may be his toy airplane. So she responds with, "You want your *airplane?*" He may nod quickly and say, "Uhuh, aipai," or some such approximation; and he is told or shown where his airplane may be found. The mother's response results in the child's more accurate pronunciation of the word. In all probability, he could do an even better job, but the particular situation does not lend itself to more specific speech work. Instead, the parent makes a mental

49

note of the word and will provide for further practice in both general and specific speech situations.

SPECIFIC APPROACH

Specific terms are used in reference to the development of each sense which enters into speech development. These are: visual, tactile, auditory, rhythmic, kinesthetic.

The *visual* aspect of the training has been discussed under Lip-reading (page 26). The child learns to use his eyes in detecting differences and similarities in lip movements, in things and people around him, in actions and interactions. Development of the sense of sight takes place through living experiences of childhood, through sense training exercises, through developmental activities such as painting, block building, experiences with books, etc., and through the incorporation of all other aspects of the training. Adequate training of the sense of sight results in better lipreading and better speech.

The *tactile* refers to the sense of touch. The child learns a great deal through feeling and touching objects and people. He can also be made more aware of his own voice and the voices of others by feeling his own face, and the faces and bodies of others, during speech and speech play. Development of the sense of touch in every possible respect makes the use of the other senses more effective.

From the earliest possible moment the deaf baby, or the deaf child should be exposed to experiences in touching and feeling. It must be done playfully and happily so the baby or the child will accept the activity as part of his normal existence.[121]

Most babies touch and pat their parents' faces, and like to cuddle close to the parents' bodies; and deaf babies do the same. Every time it happens, the parent should sing, hum, talk, laugh, —use the voice in some pleasant manner. An awareness of the "feel" of voice and other sounds need not be forced upon the child; it should develop with him. In time, he notices that when the mouth moves he feels something, and gradually he thinks of these as a unit.[56]

The *auditory* involves stimulation of the hearing mechanism as a means of making the visual and the tactile more effective and of making the deaf child more conscious of sound for better speech.[90] (See Auditory Training—Language, page 62.)

The *rhythmic* includes every type of exercise or play that could arouse in the child an awareness of the flowing movements of the body and of the relationship between such movements and speech, music, and singing. Rhythm experiences help to lay the foundation for more fluent, more normal speech.[168]

The *kinesthetic* is concerned with developing the sense of timing and of feeling in the muscles involved in speech production. The baby and the young deaf child engage in speech play as they babble, etc. The child enjoys the sensations produced as he uses his voice experimentally. Babbling and speech play should be permitted and encouraged as giving the speech muscles a chance to perform in a relaxed way, as a sort of rehearsal for later performance in learning speech production.[101]

These trends towards meaningful speech should be coordinated as much as possible and blended into the child's development as a whole. Techniques are necessary to speech development in the deaf child, but they must never become a bugaboo.

The teacher and the parent adapt methods to the child, letting one method predominate over others according to the child's enjoyment of and responses to various elements of the training.

If the adult finds that the child enjoys "listening" more than any other part of the training, she would make auditory training the center of most activities, and would use it as a wedge for the introduction, incorporation, and acceptance of other necessary elements such as lipreading, rhythm, sense training, speech imitation, etc. If the child prefers games, as much as possible should be accomplished through the medium of active play.[220]

51

THE PARENTS' CONCERNS

The parent, understandably desirous of speech and under-standing for her deaf child, may become far too concerned about the problems and difficulties that must arise, even to the degree that every real problem may be magnified. The anxieties, some-times the nature of the guidance provided for parent and child, may force the parent unwittingly to subject the child to boring, fatiguing, technical methods that inevitably do more harm than good.

There is the parent who is disturbed because her child of three or four years doesn't have a *k* sound. She has struggled—perhaps the teacher has also—and all to no avail. Further investigation shows that relatively little, if any, attention has been given to language understanding through lipreading and experiences, or to the encouragement of spontaneous speech.

The young deaf child who has been exposed to fluent natural speech in his environment and who has been encouraged to use, spontaneously and in his own way, whole words, even phrases and sentences, has a far better chance of developing the highly prized *k,* or any other speech element.

The teacher knows that the development of separate vowels and consonants is necessary to intelligible speech, but she is also aware of the fact that many vowels and consonants develop easily and spontaneously by the use of whole words that have meaning to the child, through his own imitation of those words.

Mastery of any vowels and consonants and their many combina-tions by the use of whole words, phrases, and sentences, makes the acquisition of those still to be mastered a much simpler proc-ess for teacher and child and parent.

Any speech work with isolated consonants and vowels should be in the form of speech play with emphasis on the whole idea and on the child.[146]

By the time the child is ready for more specific speech work, his speech muscles will have had much experience operating in a relaxed manner; he will have had sufficient time to acquire some understanding of language and a better idea of where speech fits into his scheme of things; and his degree of maturity will permit him to accept the more specific training which certain speech elements require.[20]

The little deaf child who has had some training in the home or in the school, or in both, may attempt words only when he can imitate a speaker. This may discourage his parents, who think that he will never talk because he doesn't do it of his own volition. The parent must be informed that many a hearing child does this, or—a parallel tendency—often has a jargon or language of his own. As the father of a little hearing child said, "Once in a while he talks English; most of the time it's some other language."

After the young deaf child learns to say one or two words well and spontaneously, he may attach one or both of them to everything he sees. This, too, is common among hearing children in the earlier stages of speech development. As the child learns to use other words spontaneously, this "improper" use of words gradually disappears.[176]

There are times when the deaf child will stop using words he has known and used at an earlier age, and the parent may become alarmed. This occurs also in the early speech development of the hearing child, although many people are not aware of it since they are not concerned so specifically with speech development as is the parent of the deaf child. The child simply has become more interested in "new" words and prefers them to the "old" ones.

The first words are not forgotten. Adults in the child's environment continue to use them as usual, and even though the child himself sees less reason for his using them at present, the words have not ceased to be a part of his environment and of him. In time, he learns to coordinate his whole vocabulary in expressing himself.

When the deaf child begins to use sentences, he, like the hearing child, uses nouns or verbs or both and usually omits prepositions, conjunctions, and pronouns. To any child, the important parts of a sentence are those words which indicate things and people and the actions revolving about both.

A complete understanding and the consistent, proper use of prepositions, conjunctions, and some pronouns demand a much longer period of training for the deaf child than the preschool years provide. The child should be exposed to all commonly used language forms in casual situations and in "lesson" periods; and as his understanding indicates a readiness, his attention might be brought to his omission of this word or that, depending on the occasion. However, drills on such words as *to* and *it* are not advised and seldom are helpful.

It is far more indicative of progress if the child says, "Go store," for "I want to go to the store," than if he could imitate the word *to* and couldn't understand the sentence in which it would be used.

If parents can be brought to understand that much of their concern is without foundation and that the so-called problems they see are frequently not real problems but positive signs of speech development, there will be fewer "errors" in their guidance of the deaf child.

The parent must also understand that the deaf child cannot acquire all the language and speech skills which are necessary to the adult while that child is still at the preschool level.[97]

SPEECH DEVELOPMENT—NOT SPEECH CORRECTION

It is important that the parent and the teacher be speech conscious, be aware of developments in speech as related to the whole child and of irregularities in the development which need extra attention. However, whether the adult is taking a general

54

or specific approach to speech, the emphasis is on *speech development* and *speech preparation,* not on *speech correction.* It is imperative that persons who are training young deaf children understand that speech development is not the same as speech correction. *What isn't there can't be corrected!*

The young deaf child's first attempts at speech, regardless of how unintelligible they may be, should be considered neither "incorrect" nor speech defects. He is learning to use his voice for specific purposes and should be encouraged to do so. He must be given time to realize that he has a voice which he may use for a purpose.

If he is exposed to well-articulated, meaningful speech, and is himself happy and relaxed, speech correction should not enter the picture until he indicates that he understands what speech is for and how to use it. And, the amount of speech correction necessary will depend on how much attention and what kind of attention was given to *speech preparation* at the preschool level.[58]

PERSONALITY AND SPEECH

The personality factor is one of the first considerations in the development of meaningful speech in the young deaf child. Speech is only a part of the whole, and its quality and its use will be commensurate with the quality of the whole child. The teacher and the parent are not merely trying to induce the child to "say words"; they wish to train him to communicate orally, so that whatever qualities, aptitudes, and intelligence he possesses may be more effective in his relation to society.[103]

Both teacher and parent must understand the influence of family life and social surroundings on the total personality of the child, and that the coordination of the vocal mechanism with the mental processes is related to developmental growth and emotional stability.[25]

There must be an understanding of the child, his limitations, his possibilities, and a respect for his individuality. Emotional reactions of the parents and the teacher which could affect the child emotionally, could also affect speech production.[69] There must be relaxation, acceptance of the child, and provision for his fundamental needs, if speech is to develop as normally as possible.[104]

The child himself should always remain more important than speech. If he meets with approval only when he says something "well," he will come to feel that speech is more important to his parents and his teacher than he is, and he may refuse to talk or cooperate in speech situations. If the pressure has been so great that he develops fear, and tries to cooperate for fear of punishment, his voice may be strained and tense, and poor speech habits may be permanently established.[70]

Speech responses will be slow as compared with responses to sense training, lipreading, and those parts of the training closer to the child's normal senses. Speech is a great part of the objective that teachers and parents hold for the child, and the desire for it must not entail any attitudes or pressures upon the child which would retard speech.[149] The child will not accept speech nor use it as well as he is able, if he has been subjected to strain, unreasonable demands, and rejection from earliest childhood.[112]

At its best, the speech of the very deaf child, even after years of training, cannot be described as "normal" in every respect.[153] Imperfections and deviations from the normal are bound to exist, but they may be minimized by making speech enjoyable to the child from the beginning.[29]

During the first months, parent and teacher strive to lay the foundation for the development of habits of attention, concentration, and cooperation which lead to social adjustment, emotional stability, and a healthful approach to speech.[161]

The child must be made to feel that he is a part of the world and that he has something useful to contribute. He must learn to understand and to feel understood. These are factors more essential in his development of meaningful speech than dry speech "lessons" involving techniques that he is not prepared to understand or accept.

The understanding he encounters and acquires in the first months through happy experiences within the family group and with others continues to grow until he exhibits a desire to speak. To accomplish this end, every adult who takes it upon himself or herself to guide the deaf child must remember that he or she is working with the child for the child, and the choice of methods and techniques will be made on that basis.

The essentials of speech development demand the removal of all unnecessary restrictions.[206] There has been considerable discussion and some disagreement about giving the deaf child of nursery years as much freedom as is the rule in some centers. Unfortunately, there still exist those persons who think that freedom in play is valuable, but that when it comes to the "lesson" a child should be strictly disciplined. It is also unfortunate that the same individuals cannot or will not see that unreasonable restrictions in one situation influence every other situation.[125]

There must be a consistency about child guidance.[134] The child who feels free in every situation, and at the same time feels secure in the knowledge that he is being guided by strong people who love him as he is, will be responsive in all situations, will want to communicate with others, will be eager to obtain and retain information, and will have a sound foundation on which favorable speech skills can be built.[128]

The synthetic approach to speech development—that is, an approach that envelops the whole child, the whole word, and the whole idea, in the whole scheme of living—leads to more normal speech with fewer "deafisms" in the speech and in the personality. And when the child is ready emotionally and intellectually for the analytical approach—that is, more technical training on *parts* of speech—he will be more accepting and cooperative, and the results will be more lasting and effective.[98]

Deaf children develop speech at different ages just as hearing children do. One deaf child should not be compared with another for his advancement in speech skills, nor judged on the basis of his large or small vocabulary. The child's achievements of this year would be compared with his own of a year ago, and his own progress from time to time would be the measuring stick for his growth.

The teacher and the parent must remember that speech is not the *all* in the life of the deaf child. The attitudes and habits necessary to the development of social skills, the understanding of language, and clear, usable speech, are established in the nursery years. Great responsibility rests upon parents and teachers.[53]

CHAPTER 6

Sense Training—Language

Sense training might be described as the springboard to communication for the young deaf child.[135] It is one of his most useful tools in learning—in developing lipreading for language understanding, in speech preparation, in reading readiness—and it is a form of learning which is play for him. He can touch, manipulate, put together, take apart, match, experiment, and attain a feeling of success through constructing forms.

The development of the senses of touch, sight, taste, smell, and sometimes hearing, which begins at the early levels through sense training, is closely related to the development of lipreading, speech, and reading, and also improves the quality of developed skills. The child's ability to observe, to match, to imitate, to experiment, leads to a proficiency in matching lip movements and speech patterns, in learning to recognize similarities and differences in printed forms, and in feeling free to express himself orally, physically, and creatively.

No parent or teacher who has an understanding of the child would underestimate the value of sense training activities in the guidance of the deaf child. In essence, speech training is sense training, auditory training is sense training, and every other special activity with which the worker is concerned for the promotion of the deaf child is related to sense training.

The parent may feel that the time spent on matching colors, objects, pictures, etc., is a waste of time, and that someone should put a stop to this "play" and "get down to business." That parent should be reminded that, in schools for hearing children, the children who have difficulty in reading, and other language problems, are taken through special programs that include the kind of sense training they should have had during the preschool years.[26]

Sense training assists in personality development. The activities often serve as means of expression and of emotional outlet, and so become tension reducers and security builders. Completion of a puzzle or form board results in a feeling of pride and achievement.

In the use of sense training exercises, all the constructive principles of parent-child relationships, teacher-child relationships, and of the child-guidance situation must be faithfully followed by the adult. Sometimes, there is a tendency to do the child's exercise for him, to try to make him understand that "this goes here" and "that goes there," instead of allowing him to satisfy his curiosity and his sense of achievement through touch, taste, smell, and sight, if he wishes to do so.

The young child will not tolerate for long an adult's interference with his exploratory measures without reacting and possibly refusing to cooperate with the adult in any learning situation. Guidance and direction are acceptable to the child, but interference is not, and the adult must recognize the fine line between the two.[19]

A teacher may say, very kindly, "This goes here, Johnny," and Johnny will proceed to remove the object and do something else with it. Early in the nursery years, reactions like that are to be expected.

However, the adult must not get the idea that the child should not be shown the "right" way. He needs to be shown, and he likes to "know how." The danger lies in how he is shown, and whether or not the adult is willing to accept his experimenting with the materials, and to continue showing him until he is

60

ready to follow directions and to get satisfaction out of doing it correctly.

Sense training for the young child doesn't start suddenly and it never stops. While the child is still in infancy, the mother plays with his toes and tells him, "That's a toe, and that's a toe." She points to his nose and to her own, to his mouth and to her own, and talks about her actions. The child, in these instances, is getting a start in matching and in lipreading and speech.

One of the first "lessons" that the parent may *do* with the child is a form of sense training. The nature of sense training activities is such that it lends itself easily to use by the untrained person. Throughout the world, there are parents who have never had the opportunity of obtaining direct guidance from a teacher, who have had to rely on correspondence, and who are using sense training exercises effectively in guiding their respective children to oral communication.

CHAPTER 7

Auditory Training—Language

Auditory training has already been referred to in relation to language and speech development as an essential part of the early education of the deaf child. Recent scientific research leaves little doubt in the minds of professional workers regarding the existence of residual hearing in the majority of deaf children.[90] The degree and importance of this hearing have often been underestimated on the basis of negative results from a hearing test, or because the child made little or no response to auditory training.

As the experienced person in this field knows, the responses to sound, even among severely deaf children, may vary greatly from child to child; and the rate of progress in auditory training also varies considerably at and beyond certain stages. The degree to which auditory training helps the deaf child in speech and lipreading development also differs, although an efficient program, carried out over a sufficiently long period of time, should benefit the child to some degree.[95]

The child who is trained to use his residual hearing to the fullest extent develops a better understanding of the relationships between sounds and objects, sounds and actions, sounds and people; and he begins to associate the sounds of speech with the language he has learned through lipreading. This inevitably leads to better speech and a more comprehensive grasp of language.[88]

The teacher or parent training the child's hearing will realize that the process must be adapted to the individual child and varied according to the progressive effect upon the whole child as his hearing is affected. Techniques in auditory training are designed not only to stimulate response to sound, but to improve the child's whole response to his environment. Workers must be constantly ready to evaluate the effect of the training on the understanding of language, on the quality of voice and speech, on the ability to concentrate, on the uses of all the senses, and on the whole personality.[154]

Auditory training over a period of time enables the parent and the teacher to estimate more accurately the nature and degree of the hearing loss and its relation to the child's future education. While the teacher and the parent may be guided by results of previous tests and may plan the educational programs accordingly, they must realize that, whatever these tests may indicate, the auditory training should be begun and continued. First tests could prove misleading, as responses frequently change over a period of months.

It is helpful for parent and teacher to have had some experience in watching the responses of hearing children to sounds and to speech. A hearing baby who is absorbed in some activity that interests him may make no appreciable response even to a loud sound produced directly behind him.

One story of a hearing baby's response to sound might be of interest to parents and teachers who encounter problematical situations in testing and training the hearing of young deaf children. Several deaf children were being tested before a large audience. A hearing baby was included in the demonstration.

The latter sat on his mother's lap playing with a toy. The teacher beat drums and blew whistles near him; the baby paid absolutely no attention to her or the sounds, but went on playing with his toy. During a pause, a baby in the audience suddenly gurgled. The hearing baby being tested looked up immediately and in the general direction of the source of the sound.

This coincidence was most enlightening to the audience in regard to what is involved in hearing tests for any young child. To expect a standard set of responses from all deaf children provides only a false basis on which to make a diagnosis.[52]

A deaf child may respond to a sound one day and then apparently ignore it on other days. Parents, teachers, and other workers are constantly being confronted with such situations. Some of the reasons might be increased loss of hearing, either temporary or progressive; emotional reaction to the parent, to the teacher, or to the situation, which could result in the child's refusing to hear or to respond; boredom with the frequent repetition of a sound that has become so clear to him that he sees no reason for responding every time he hears it; climatic conditions; physical well-being or fatigue.

There are reasons, either real or psychological, for a child's response or lack of it, and while it is wise to put some effort into finding such reasons and causes, it is most unwise to allow them to become excuses to halt the auditory training or to cause emotional disturbances in the parent.

RESULTS MAY BE SLOW

The results of auditory training will be more effective if parent and teacher realize that the training may be a slow process. There are extremists who say, "Give the child auditory training; make him hear. Do not teach him to lipread, for if he uses lipreading, he will not use his hearing. If he will not listen, do not respond to him." This is as preposterous as telling a blind child that he cannot have his dinner unless he uses his eyes to read the name of the food. Deafness presents enough problems without our adding to them by trying to "make" the child hear.

The very young child has no conception of what "listening"

means and it becomes necessary to give him a pleasant and enjoyable first experience of it.

In the case of the very young deaf child, the unaided voice should be used at first. The young child who cannot understand the reason for wearing earphones may permit the parent or the teacher to talk near his ear in a normal tone of voice. Many deaf children will accept the wearing of earphones within a short period of time, but there are those who need more time, sometimes months, and both parent and teacher must be prepared for this possibility and be willing to give the child time to adjust to the use of earphones and to amplified sound.

If the child rejects all auditory training consistently, even violently, the adult should compare this attitude with the child's reactions to other phases of the training, and should try to determine whether the rejection is for auditory training only, or involves other factors such as parent-child relationships.

Sometimes the child who has some usable hearing will react in an extreme degree to amplified sound. The parent and the teacher have to take precautions with this child. He has difficulty in adjusting to the sounds he hears—so strange to him!—and during the early weeks of training he is not able to take much. If he will use the headset, he should be watched carefully for signs of nervousness and fatigue, and the periods of training should be short, and increased very gradually.

Auditory training should be offered whenever the child will accept it, not only during formal lesson periods, but when the child is completely relaxed, as during his rest periods. Parents have found that they get good results when lying beside the child on the bed before he goes to sleep at night, when he is at ease, and when his whole body is touching that of the speaker so that he is more aware of vibration. Auditory training is more effective when it is combined with lipreading, sense training, speech preparation and other interesting activities.

A WEARABLE AID WHEN POSSIBLE

The child who responds well to auditory training, and whose voice and speech show improvement after auditory training with an amplifier, should be considered a candidate for a wearable aid.[138] Any child who will accept such an aid, and who obviously could benefit from one, should have the opportunity of using it through as much of the day as possible for him.[122]

PROGRESS THROUGH AUDITORY TRAINING

After the child becomes more conscious of sound and learns to recognize certain speech sounds—whether he hears them or is aware of them only through vibration—his lipreading and his speech show improvement.[75] He imitates the patterns "heard" and his speech is more normal in rhythm and accent. He is more aware of his environment as a whole, as this additional sense is put into use. Psychologically he is benefited, and as he becomes more conscious of sound he behaves more and more like a hearing child. He begins to notice how hearing persons react when they listen to a sound which he also hears, and he patterns his responses after theirs, even though he may hear it in a different way.

Auditory training, well-organized for the individual child and maintained over a period of years from the time the child is very young, not only helps to make the speech and language more normal, but, what is more important, makes the child feel more like his hearing brothers and sisters.[156]

CHAPTER 8

Reading Readiness—Language

Reading skills are vital to the deaf person throughout life. The ability to read well puts him in touch with his world, helps him to develop his personality, and gives him an unfailing sense of recreation. Before he can understand the language of the printed page, he must have learned to understand language in its other forms—spoken language, the language of experience through play and activity in everyday life—and to have some conception of the role of language in society, and its place in his life.

This preparation or readiness for reading begins in the nursery years, long before the child has any awareness of the printed word. Every experience that the child has had from birth comes with him to his first true reading experiences in the schoolroom, and the nature and number of those experiences will have a definite bearing on the ease or difficulty with which he attempts the printed page.

The educator knows, and the parent must be brought to know, that reading is a basic tool subject throughout the school years. Difficulties in reading will retard the child in every other subject. The deaf child's progress in reading tends to be much slower than that of the hearing child, and accordingly his progress in other areas is held back. His progress may be accelerated by laying a good *foundation for reading,* early.[60]

It would be unfortunate·if, in the attempt to develop reading skills, the young deaf child were forced into the formal reading situation at too early an age. The child cannot be developed into a better adult, nor made to mature more rapidly, by making him behave as an adult; nor will he be made a better reader by "teaching reading" to him before he is ready, simply because he is a deaf child.

Reading difficulties are based to a large degree on language difficulties. The deaf child in the grades may be able to say certain words in a passage, may recognize them as meaning a particular object or activity, but he is not reading unless he can get the whole idea from the passage well enough to answer and ask questions regarding the content. If he cannot perform at this level, the teacher, even in the literature or social studies lesson, must turn the lesson into one on language, and the child will probably take two years to cover the work of one grade.

There is no royal road to reading skills for the deaf child, and problems certainly do arise for even the best prepared. However, if a better language background is laid in the nursery years and if consideration has been given to all factors contributing to reading readiness, the difficulties in the grades should be fewer and more easily dealt with, and the whole progress of the deaf child could be speeded up.[117]

The hearing child has approximately six years in which to assimilate knowledge and experiences through living, before he is exposed to a reading program. He has learned to understand what people are talking about, to recognize the relationship between spoken words and activities and people, to observe actions and reactions among people, to use spoken language himself, and to express himself in many ways. His parents read books to him, give him the names of things and people about him, and expose him to all the experiences that his environment permits. These are all essential reading experiences which must precede experiences with printed words.

Studies have shown that mental alertness, good health, social adjustment, and emotional stability, ability to "perceive sequence" and to reorganize ideas, good work habits, ability to concentrate, sensory ability, adequate motor control, and a keen interest in learning, as well as an ability to understand in oral situations any words that might appear in the first reading books, are all important requisites for reading. "In general, a child is ready for reading when his total development is sufficient to enable him to engage effectively in the various activities involved in learning to read. However, it should be understood that lack of ability in any of the elements that comprise reading readiness may tend to retard the *rate of progress* in learning to read." [83]

Proficiency in these fields must be attained before the young deaf child can be expected to read. The fact that the child is deaf cannot justify the teacher's nor the parent's attempts to "teach reading" before the child is equipped with the tools that will make reading possible. Such attempts are at best superficial and harmful.

The deaf child must be physically ready before reading is introduced to him. His eyes, which are of such special importance to him, must not be overtaxed, and the eyes of a very young child are not able to make the visual discrimination necessary for word recognition and the reading of phrases and sentences.

Emotional readiness and maturity are equally important. The deaf child has to make adjustments beyond those of the hearing child, and further pressures, such as being expected to read while he is still at the preschool level, will increase his adjustment problems. Early reading, before the child is ready, may cause tensions that produce confusion in reading, defective focusing of the eyes, and a general retardation which may not appear until the child is past the preschool years, when both reading and emotional problems are much more difficult to resolve.

Although no formal reading program for the preschool deaf child should be pursued, the wise teacher and parent must recognize the need for an adequate reading readiness program. When the printed word enters of necessity into such a program, the adult in charge must employ it with due regard to the distinction between reading and reading readiness. The deaf child cannot be expected to read younger than the hearing child, but he should be, as early as possible, exposed to a reading readiness program that is directed towards his understanding the spoken language associated with all his experiences—lipreading, speech, sense training, auditory training, creative activities, free play, and activities with the people he encounters at home, in nursery school, and in the community.

Reading cannot function as a social and intellectual tool until there is understanding of language through experiences and lipreading. Parents, especially, should not be misled into thinking that lipreading and reading are things apart, for they are closely related.

Before he is introduced to the printed word, the child should have a working knowledge of that word in relation to everyday life. As the child is led from the known to the unknown and is taught to use the familiar (lipreading and experiences) to help him interpret the unfamiliar (the printed word), he is being soundly *prepared* for reading.

The word "reading" is frequently misused, especially in respect to deaf children. One must not get the impression that being able to recognize a number of isolated words is "reading," nor that the child who can recognize a number of words in a particular situation is able to read. Word recognition is merely a part of the reading readiness program. Furthermore, the degree to which the child understands that word and the contribution such recognition will make to his future reading skills will depend on how well he is able to understand it by lipreading in the situations of everyday life, and how broad a concept of that word he possessed before he encountered it in printed form.[71]

The child who understands the printed word before him will not only be able to connect it with the corresponding picture or object in the immediate situation, but, consciously or unconsciously, will remember other experiences which he has had with that word. The teacher and the parent aim for this kind of recognition. The more experience the child is able to take to the printed page, the faster he will interpret the printed words; he will feel more secure about the new situation; he will be stimulated to learn more words in this way; and he will be getting another and a broader concept of language.

The language understanding that makes for good reading is developed by experiences with language through lipreading in real situations and from developmental growth, not from printed words.

WHEN AND WHERE TO START

The parent often wonders when the child should be exposed to printed words. Actually he is exposed to them from the time he is first read to from books. He may become interested in them before the adult thinks of introducing them. This interest of his, however, must not be interpreted as a signal to begin "reading" in the schoolroom sense.

There are three-year-olds and four-year-olds who have gone to their parents and teachers with printed pages, wanting to know "what they say." Certainly no teacher or parent will deprive the child of an explanation. Indeed, this situation offers an excellent opportunity for constructive talking to the child and for encouraging his interests. But the adult must not immediately go about setting up a program that centers around word-recognition. Most three- and four-year-olds are not ready to understand printed words, and although printed words may begin to appear for him in more and more places, no emphasis should be placed on those words. The child is merely being exposed to them as a means of making him conscious of their existence. Later he will become aware of their relationship to things in his life, and still later will be able to interpret them in the light of those relationships. If the deaf child of three or four is forced to spend a large part of the daily training in the superficial performance of identifying certain words, then other activities that are much more necessary to his total development, and in particular to his future reading ability, are being neglected.

In the event of a three- or four-year-old exhibiting a desire to find out about a printed word, the teacher and the parent should try to satisfy the child's curiosity through familiar channels. The child may be curious about the word printed below the picture of the boy. The adult would tell the child that it says *John,* and that the boy's name is *John.* "You are *Billy.* That is *John.* This is *John,* and that says *John.*" If the child is still attentive and interested, the adult might get a pencil and two cardboard strips, and print *John* on one strip and *Billy* on the other. "This says *Billy.* That says *John.*" The adult might get a snapshot of Billy and clip the name to the picture, and place the other strip on the page of the book.

In such an instance the child is getting more practice in lipreading, in matching a printed form to a picture, and, although his understanding of the printed form itself is at a minimum and is entirely dependent upon his understanding through lipreading, another concept of language is taking root.

Other simple printed words may be introduced gradually in connection with lipreading, speech, and auditory training. But they should be introduced as casually as a new picture would be hung upon the wall, with the emphasis on the lipreading, the pictures, and the activities that revolve about the word, not on any attempt to get the child to interpret the printed form.

Action verbs are frequently used by teachers in the early word recognition periods, especially with those children who are interested in activity and have therefore easily learned to lipread such words. In the lesson where such words are being used for lipreading and speech practice, the printed form of two or three might be introduced. The child has already learned to watch the speaker's face, and as the adult says, "Run," and holds up the printed word on a card, the child, although probably interested in this new approach, is still getting the idea through lipreading. And he should be permitted to do so.

The adult must not expect the child to stand and study the word for minutes, to become frustrated, and even insecure and frightened, when he could be led to understand the printed word through his already acquired lipreading ability and related experiences. Once more, parent and teacher are reminded of the principle of leading the child from the familiar to the less familiar.

In time, as the child encounters a few printed words in connection with other lessons, he begins to realize that there are differences in printed forms just as there are differences in spoken forms, and in colors and forms used in sense training. And he begins to notice that, when a certain word is said, a particular printed form appears at the same time. The deaf child must be given time to make such identifications for himself without any force from the adult.

Usually, by the time the child is ready for Grade I, he understands that everything has a name that may be put down on paper or on a blackboard, just as everything has a name that is recognizable on the lips. He may also realize that actions and activities may not only be spoken of, but may be printed about. This realization is a great stride towards reading, even though the child is as yet able to interpret but few printed words without the aid of lipreading. Reading readiness has been established in his total development through the preschool years as one more experience by which to enrich other experiences, one more way of expressing himself—not a "subject" apart from living.

In the presentation and use of printed words, phrases, and short sentences, the adult is once more reminded that the symbols on the little strips of paper must not stand alone, as abstractions. Every printed form used is related to conversation, books, pictures, and other interesting activities, even to the five-year-old. There is a constant attempt to broaden the concept of any language form presented, and for this reason lipreading, speech, auditory training, reading readiness, and other means of language development must be combined as much as possible.

Printed forms must make their appearance as whole words rather than as single letters of the alphabet, just as whole words must be used in beginning lipreading and speech. The whole word, spoken or printed, can be illustrated, while a letter of the alphabet cannot; and in reading readiness, as in other phases of the training, the deaf child must be given a concept which can be made as concrete as possible and which he can understand in relation to living.[61]

Words are matched to objects and pictures, and to corresponding words, just as in sense training identical pictures and objects were matched. The parent and teacher will find that the child who has had ample experience with sense training activities, as well as with lipreading, will learn to recognize much more easily the similarities and differences among printed words.

Later on, simple phrases, such as *a big ball, a red house,* and others with which the child has become familiar through lipreading, are introduced in printed form. In time, the child learns to match them to corresponding pictures and to corresponding printed phrases. Later still, short, simple sentences are used in a like manner.

Some deaf children, by the time they are ready for Grade I, recognize a number of words, phrases, and sentences; others may recognize very few or none. Differences among even the most intelligent children will be noted. The progress of the deaf child and his readiness for Grade I should not be measured by the number of printed words he is able to recognize, but rather by the requisite preliminaries to reading which he has acquired through the previous reading readiness program set up and followed by his parents and teacher.

The value of reading readiness at the preschool level should not be vitiated by making printed forms the core of the training.

The deaf child at the preschool level can be *prepared* for reading; he will not read.

The printed form, introduced at the "right" time for the individual child, can be a source of stimulation and interest in learning, and although it is essential that language understanding through lipreading and experiences come first, this new experience with words can be an accelerating factor in the total language development.

In setting up a reading readiness program for the young deaf child, parent and teacher will adhere to the basic principles of learning and teaching: to proceed from attitudes to habits to skills, to establish impression before expression, and to adapt techniques to the individual personality. They will not make the error of molding the child to a reading program that is far beyond his capacity to comprehend.

The parent and the teacher who can establish language understanding through lipreading and experiences which the deaf child must have will know how to prepare the child for future reading skills without destroying the developmental values that a reading readiness program should have.[175]

75

CHAPTER 9

Developmental Activities—Language

Developmental activities include all those activities which help the child develop himself through living. If a teacher or parent knew nothing about special techniques for the deaf, but was well trained in nursery school procedures, she could provide even the preschool deaf child with a very necessary part of the foundation for future academic training.

Whether the child is deaf or not, the avenue of learning for him, along which he makes his way from childhood to adulthood, is through play and other experience.[220] Since the problems of deafness could make this progress more difficult and complex, play and experiences that especially provide impressions and expression would be especially relevant to the young deaf child's development.[91]

Observation of the child in all situations—play, games, painting, etc.—gives the parent and the teacher a better understanding of the child—his aptitudes, his problems, how far along in his development he may be, in what direction he appears to be going —and suggest what may be done to direct and redirect his energies for healthier and more positive growth.[50] Developmental activities, serving as a means of revealing problems, also serve as one means in resolving them.[45]

The fact that the deaf child during the first years is deprived of one outlet for expression—speech—could indicate an especially urgent need for more expression through the other means at his disposal. Provision for more interests, and outlets that are well-chosen in relation to his needs and personality, could help to alleviate frustration, as a "stop-gap" until the time when the child is able to express himself through speech.

As the child is exposed to many activities, he learns to participate with others, to achieve some measure of success in each activity, and to develop the special aptitude to the greatest possible degree.[62] This helps to lay the foundation for a more versatile adolescence and maturity. The child discovers not only what he can do best, but that he can do many things.[94] He does not stop painting because Johnny's pictures are more acceptable to the teacher; nor does he scorn Johnny's attempts at woodworking because his own are more acceptable to teacher and parent. The adult must not be responsible for adopting these destructive attitudes and imposing them upon the child.[169] Teacher and parent guide the child and measure his success both by the amount of effort he puts into an activity and by the amount of enjoyment he gets out of it, not by comparing his work with that of some other child.[49]

Language through lipreading and speech is related to these activities, and, although the value of the exercise of language should not be destroyed nor lessened by being turned into a speech or lipreading lesson in the formal sense, there are many times when the situation lends itself naturally to talking to the child. Teachers and parents discover that the deaf child's interest in the activities stimulates his desire to watch lips and to attempt further expression through his own speech.

Language grows through dramatic play, games, excursions, creative activities, music and rhythm, and experiences with books.[79] Such developmental activities are adapted to the child in the home, in the neighborhood, in the hearing nursery, or in the nursery school for deaf children. They are the need of all children, a common bond between the deaf child and the hearing child.

The teacher and the parent with vision, who make the child's world rich in experience and opportunity for expression, determine to a great degree the nature of the child's future.[74]

"We define the child in development by Goethe's words as 'a stamped form, developing itself through living.' In other words, a personality nucleus is supposedly inborn, but life directs the development of this nucleus, stimulating certain parts, suppressing others. The educator with this viewpoint must first become very familiar with the nucleus of the child's personality. If the child shows extreme motor activities, it will go against the child's nucleus always to keep him quiet. But, on the other hand, the motor activities of the child can be directed; they can be realized in sports emphasizing the child's feeling of his own body; they can be realized in games emphasizing the child's social relationships; they can be realized in the child's creative activities. The educator has the task of bringing into accord dispositions and aims, the 'what' and the 'for what.' The 'what' of the child's dispositions has to be explored carefully, observing his thought and expression. The 'for what' should be a mixture of the educator's ideals and the child's possibilities." [220]

PART 2

Activities
for Language
Development

CHAPTER 10

Sense Training Activities
for Language Development

Teacher and parent must present the sense training exercises suggested here in whatever order seems best for the individual child, taking into consideration the child's age, what the "average" child of that age might be expected to do, the child's muscular coordination, and his attention span. Both teacher and parent aim at helping the child to develop skills in every part of the sense training program. However, through observation of the child during play, creative activities, and during free play with sense training materials at other times, the adult will discover the child's aptitudes and preferences—whether the child appears to be most interested in color, form, or other element—and will guide the child sensibly and naturally from the more interesting to the less interesting, from the simple to the more difficult.

The success attained in sense training will depend to a large extent on the adult's willingness to respect the child's individuality and to recognize his preferences and his requirements as more important than any arbitrary set of standards which the adult may have in mind.

SENSE OF SIGHT

A. MATCHING

  (1) MATCH OBJECTS

    a. Match objects identical in every respect.

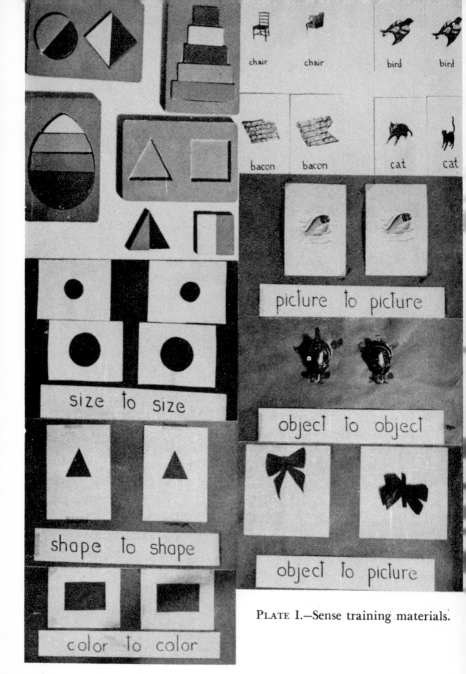

chair   chair   bird   bird

bacon   bacon   cat   cat

picture to picture

size to size

object to object

shape to shape

object to picture

color to color

PLATE I.—Sense training materials.

    b. Match objects of different size.
    c. Match objects of different color.
    d. Match objects of different size and color.
    e. Match objects (any of above) using tactile method.

The matching of objects usually comes first, since the child tends to be more interested in a form that he can hold and manipulate. The simplest exercise involves the matching of two objects that are identical in every respect. Two bright blue balls and two bright red airplanes might be used, or pairs of other objects which would be of interest to the child. (Plate I)

With a child who seems to be confused by colors, the adult would use objects all of one color; that is, every object used in the first exercises might be blue, later on, another set of red ones might be used; and so on until the child has had more experience with colors and colored objects.

The primary aim is that the child learn to match the objects, and in most instances the same color helps the child to match pairs of objects more quickly.

When the exercise is presented for the first time, or even for the first few times, the child may want to feel the objects, to roll or push them, or even taste them. If he has had experience with similar objects in play situations, he may not wish to spend time experimenting with them. When materials are very new to a child, the parent and the teacher must be prepared to allow for his desire to explore and experiment.

The adult might place a ball and an airplane on a surface near the child (on the floor, on the table, or elsewhere) and the corresponding objects in her lap. She might take the ball from her lap, hold it up, and say, "This is a ball, Johnny. It's a ball. Let's find the other ball."

The child may pick up the other ball, or he might choose the airplane. If he chooses the latter (and this is quite probable), the teacher will show the child what she means by indicating or picking up the other ball. Then she would put both balls together and say, "This is a ball, and this is a ball." A similar procedure would be used with the airplanes.

Johnny may not watch for long and, at first, may watch the objects rather than the speaker. The adult must be prepared for this reaction and be willing to accept it as the natural thing for the child to do. After all, the deaf child of two or three can understand what to do with a toy, if only to handle it, while as yet he cannot understand why he should watch the adult. Furthermore, at this stage, learning to match the objects is of the first importance.

The exercise may be repeated, and the second attempt may result in Johnny's handing the adult the correct object. The number of identical objects used in a lesson is increased as the child grasps the idea of matching.

Before long, objects that differ in size only may be introduced. Two balls, one large and one small; two airplanes, one large and one small; two shoes, one large and one small; and other familiar objects would be presented in a manner similar to that described for identical objects.

As pairs of objects are matched, the child is confronted with more and more differences. In the first stages, it is preferable to use objects that differ in one respect only. If the two balls differ in size, they should remain the same in color or design; if the colors differ, then the sizes would be the same. This is not so imperative with the child of four or five years, but with the younger child, it makes the transitions easier, and he can be guided gradually to observe small differences in objects, an observation that has a bearing on lipreading development.

Whenever possible, without annoying the child or interfering with his execution of the exercise, the teacher and parent talk about the objects. The name of the object is repeated frequently.

It doesn't matter if it is described as a big ball, a red airplane, or just as a ball, or an airplane, so long as it is spoken of in short, simple sentences or phrases.

Sometimes it is wiser to refrain from talking, as when the attempt to talk entails too much movement in order to get the child's attention, with the undesirable results of an annoyed child and an irritable, fatigued adult. The child, if given the opportunity of doing the job he sets out to do, will get the idea of watching the speaker more and more consistently when an object is presented.

When the child becomes accustomed to matching, after a good relationship has been established between him and the adult, the tactile approach may be introduced. Occasionally, as the adult presents an object, she places the child's hand on her cheek and talks about the object. This helps to draw more attention to the speaker's face and lips and is a step in speech preparation. This should be done as casually as holding up an object.

> f. Lipread name of object using tactile; match object to corresponding object.
> g. Lipread object without tactile; match to corresponding object.
> h. Lipread object using tactile and auditory; match to corresponding object.
> i. Lipread object using auditory, no tactile; match to corresponding object.

As the child enjoys numerous experiences in matching objects in incidental and more formal situations, and gets practice in placing his hand on the speaker's face, the habit of lipreading is taking root. Imitation of speech may have begun also. The tactile and the auditory may be introduced into the activities connected with lipreading and matching, but only at the rate at which the child can accept such variations.

85

The adult holds up one ball, places the child's hand on her cheek, and says, "This is a ball, Jimmy," and pointing to the other ball says, "This is another ball." Then, using the tactile again, she would talk about the ball she has, asking, "Where is the other ball?" or saying, "Give me the other ball." If the child doesn't respond, she might hold out her hand and repeat, "Give me the other ball."

This rudimentary preparation of the child for lipreading through matching should be pursued both with and without the tactile approach. Although the tactile approach is of tremendous value to the child and an essential part of his training, he also needs experience without it, and there is danger that its overuse might cause the child to reject it.

The matching exercise might be varied again by placing the child's hand on the speaker's cheek, talking about the object while he watches, and then repeating the word or phrase near his ear. When earphones are used, then tactile, auditory, and visual approaches may be combined. The child may watch for lipreading, may feel the speaker's face for speech, and listen as the adult speaks into the microphone.

Occasionally, the adult might hold up an object, and while the child listens in his earphones, could cover her mouth and say the word into the microphone. Since he is a deaf child, she will not expect him to "hear," but he should have the experience of listening for speech patterns.

Since the child is able to see the object in the adult's hand, he will be able, in all probability, to get the corresponding object immediately, regardless of how much he "heard." But the exercise still has value in furnishing him practice in listening in relation to something which *he* can do.

Whenever this variant of the exercise is used, it should be followed up immediately by the speaker repeating the words as the child watches the speaker's whole face.

PLATE II.—Matching object to picture with lipreading.

(2) Matching Object to Picture
   j. Match object to picture (added differences).

Matching objects to pictures increases the child's understanding of the relationships between pictured objects and real ones. It is common to see a very young child try to pick a pictured object from a page or card. He expects to pick it up just as he picked up the real object. Matching of objects to pictures helps the child to understand more about his environment.

The first exercise would involve the use of a few objects and identical pictured ones to correspond with the real objects. In later exercises, more pictures and objects would be matched, with gradual changes in color, size, and possibly in contour, according to the objects.

The child learns to connect a big ball with the small one in the picture, a red chair in the room with the green one in the picture, the pictured door of the doll house with the door in his home, the three-dimensional object in his hand with the flat one on the paper.

Lipreading and the use of the tactile and auditory approaches would be incorporated into the lessons according to the readiness of the child, and in a manner similar to that prescribed for the matching of objects. (Plate II)

Parents are encouraged to supplement the nursery school training, or whatever specific training the child is getting, by exposing the child to pictures and objects at home. Pictures of his toothbrush, facecloth, soap, towel, etc., would be pinned or pasted in the bathroom below each of those articles. Pictures of the clothing in each of his drawers might be tacked to the outside of the drawer or near by so the child can match each piece of clothing he or his mother takes out of the drawer to the pictured article. Pictures of food might be put up somewhere in the kitchen.

The more he practices matching picture to object in such situations, the more success he will have in the lesson situation.

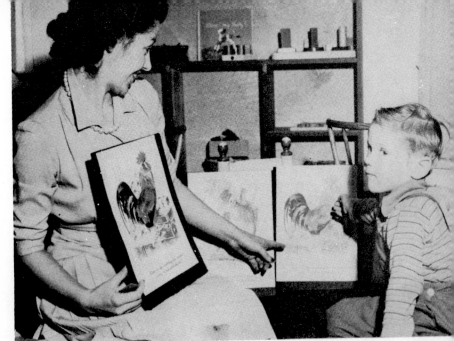

PLATE III.—Adult guiding child in picture-matching.

(3) MATCHING PICTURE TO PICTURE
k. *Match pictures that are identical.*
l. *Match pictures that illustrate objects of different size.*
m. *Match pictures of objects that differ in color.*
n. *Match pictures that differ in color and size.*
o. *Match pictures that are increasingly more detailed and complicated.*

The first pictures matched are simple, clearly defined, and identical. There should be just a single object illustrated on each card. Gradually, the child learns to match more complicated pictures that include several objects and people. (Plates III and IV)

If the first pictures presented to the young deaf child for matching purposes included many people, many activities, and a wealth of detail, he would tend to spend time investigating each of the objects or people illustrated instead of matching the identical pictures, or he would be completely confused about what is wanted of him when the adult tries to have him match such pictures. The child should have plenty of opportunity to explore pictures in books at other times during the day, but in the specific training situations he needs to be guided systematically from the simple to the more complicated, and should not be expected to match just *any* pictures which the adult may have on hand.[5]

These matching exercises should include some activity that will lend interest and variety. The child might enjoy matching pictures to corresponding ones which have been placed across the room; he might enjoy searching through a pile of pictures for the right one; or he might like to "find" corresponding pictures in boxes or drawers. It is worth the time involved in the child's having to go and get a picture, or to look for a picture, if the activity helps to maintain his interest.

PLATE IV.—Child matching pictures without guidance.

(4) Lipreading with Picture Matching

p. *Lipread name of object illustrated, use tactile; match to corresponding picture.*

q. *Lipread, using tactile and auditory; match picture to picture.*

r. *Lipread, without tactile or auditory; match.*

s. *Lipread, using auditory; match.*

Lipreading as it is introduced in these matching exercises would appear to render error on the child's part almost impossible. This is as it should be, and is important in the transitory stage. The child is being introduced gradually to lipreading, is getting an unconscious grasp of language through lipreading at the same time that he is enjoying experiences with colorful, interesting materials. He must not be expected to lipread nor imitate the names of objects at once.

So much repetition is required that the teacher and the parent find themselves constantly thinking up new and different ways of putting across the same idea. Some children take much longer than others to understand that they must watch the speaker in these matching situations. Since the child must not be forced to watch nor to conform to adult standards of behavior, the whole situation must be made so stimulating and interesting that the child will naturally accept the techniques devised by the adult for the promotion of language development.

Sometimes the use of "suspense" or "mystery" in the lesson results in more attention to the speaker's face. A few pictures might be placed on the table, the corresponding ones on the adult's lap. The adult might take one in hand, pretending to hide a very special picture from the child, and say, with playful expressions, before showing the picture to the child, "I have a ball, Johnny. A pretty ball." Then she would flash the picture quickly and match it quickly to the one on the table. She would use a similar procedure with the other pictures, talking about each before showing it to the child. If he wants to match them at once, he should be permitted to do so.

When this has been done, the adult might ask the child for each picture, sometimes using the tactile method, sometimes without it. When the child selects the correct picture, with or without help, he might place it in a box which the teacher or parent has given to him.

Simple game situations do a great deal to hold the attention and interest, especially if they are not overdone. The child quickly catches on to the fact that an adult is going through this or that action or "antic," not because she is enjoying it with him, but because she is trying to place emphasis on something else, outside and beyond him and the sheer enjoyment of the game. If he realizes this, much of the value of the picture matching and the game is lost. Unfortunately, often the adult doesn't perceive as quickly as she should the child's understanding of these situations. In that case, the matching just goes on as a task from day to day, and becomes more and more boring to the child.

Since picture matching can become so boring and devoid of interest for the child who has to have some work in it day after day, the adult must not only be on the alert for new ways of presenting picture matching for language growth but also must be able to enjoy the child and herself in whatever approach she may choose.

Lotto games, where individual pictures of objects are to be matched to corresponding pictures on a cardboard chart, furnish another variation in picture matching. (Plate V) Teacher and parent may make their own charts and cards to include objects that are not included in the lotto games available in stores.[160]

B. COLOR

The child's interest in color must be developed before he is introduced to the lipreading of color names, or prepared to say the colors and to recognize the beauty of color in daily surroundings.

The little child finds enjoyment in going from room to room or from object to object within one room, matching a color in his clothing, or in a favorite toy that he holds, to a corresponding color in the furniture, the walls, the dishes, the curtains, etc. He likes to do this when out walking, while looking at picture books, and at other times.

Colorful toys can be used to advantage. Three or four toy cups, each a different color, might be placed before the child. Bows of colored yarn or ribbon would be handed to the child, one at a time. The blue bow would be placed in the blue cup, the red bow in the red cup, etc. The child has to be shown what is expected of him, and, according to the individual child, more or less time will be required to master the operation. The child may not be interested in little bows, and in that case the adult will find it necessary to get the color matching idea across in another way. The child should not be forced to use bows if he doesn't like them.

The exercise may be varied by using colored beads or colored blocks, which could be dropped into boxes of corresponding color. Sometimes the child likes to pour colored water into painted tin cans of corresponding color.

If the child's coordination permits it, beads might be strung on colored laces. The child would be given three laces, a red one, a blue one, and a yellow one. There would be three beads from which to choose—a red one, a yellow one, and a blue one. The child would be guided in putting the red lace through the red bead, the yellow lace through the yellow bead, etc.

Tops of matchboxes might be painted or covered with colored paper. Then toy cars of corresponding color might be rolled into each cover as a car into a garage. Or toy cars and toy airplanes might be rolled onto pieces of colored cardboard on the floor.

The adult might outline and color a network of "roads" on a

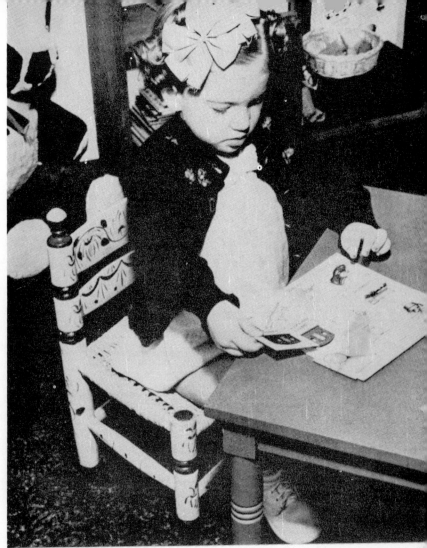

Courtesy John Tracy Clinic

PLATE V.—Picture matching, using commercially available Lotto Games.

large piece of cardboard, and the child could play at "driving the car" on the road which is colored to correspond with the car.

There are color boards which resemble puzzles and which may be bought or made. The simple form board might have one section lined with blue, into which the blue pieces would be fitted; the section lined with red would be filled with the red pieces of the puzzle. (Plate I)

Form boards that have a single object insert for each base may be used in color matching exercises. For example, a blue ball cut-out would fit into the board with the blue base and the round cut-out. In this case, the child is matching not only color but also shape.

Fortunately, these little form boards are easily made, since the parent and the teacher usually find that there are not enough simple ones available in stores to give the deaf child the repetition he needs. The object may be drawn on a piece of plywood about four inches square, and cut out with a coping saw. Then a piece of stiff cardboard would be glued firmly to the base of the plywood square. Both square and cut-out would be painted the required color. When completed, the cut-out fits easily into the base from which it was originally cut.[183]

Throughout the color matching, the adult gives the child opportunity to use his hands, to observe, to finish what he has started, and to study and concentrate on the activity. She talks to him as much as possible, and encourages him to watch her as she talks about each color. The tactile and auditory methods are combined with lipreading and matching as they were in the matching of pictures and objects.

C. SHAPE

The type of form board just described under *Color* may be used for practice and experience with various shapes. Form boards and puzzles composed of a single object or shape per board should come first, more difficult and complicated ones

PLATE VI.—Deaf two-year-old completing one-piece puzzle.

being introduced gradually. Some parents who have attempted this work have made the error of presenting puzzles far beyond the comprehension, coordination, and attention span of their respective children. (Plate VI)

There are available in stores many colorful puzzles, ranging from single object inserts to more complicated ones depicting children's activities and nursery rhymes. The adult usually finds it necessary to supplement those available in stores. The proper use of puzzles and form boards gives the child an early and enjoyable start in sense training, lipreading, and other aspects of language.

Geometric shapes cut from colored paper and pasted on cards are attractive to most children and serve as material for matching shapes. From a sheet of red paper, the adult might cut out two squares, two circles, two diamonds, two rectangles, two triangles, two polygons, etc. Each shape would be mounted on an individual card. For variety, one set of shapes might be mounted on cards and the other set on a large chart.

The child who gets sufficient practice with these shapes, and continues to show interest, learns that circles match each other, that triangles go together, regardless of what color they may be or whether they are large or small.

At first, the two circles would be identical as to color and size, the triangles identical in the same respects, and likewise for other shapes used. Gradually, the colors are changed so that the child finds himself matching a blue triangle to a purple triangle. In some cases, there may be some sign of conflict about the situation. The child may offer resistance to the problem of whether to match color or shape. He may start out by matching the blue triangle to the blue circle. Patience and continued direction on the part of the teacher and parent result in the child's learning to match the shapes rather than the colors in the appropriate situation.

As the child becomes more adept at matching shapes, assorted

98

colors and sizes are introduced, and the child learns to place all the triangles in one row regardless of size or color, all the squares in another row, etc.

Geometric solids made of natural wood, unpainted, are useful in learning to match shapes. Every parent and teacher should provide a set of these for the children. The adult may use them as identical objects were used in matching. She would place a few in a box and give them to the child, while keeping the matching ones in her lap. She would hold up one and the child would find the corresponding one in the box. The number of different shapes from which the child would have to choose would be increased as his understanding of the situation and his attention span would permit.

D. MEMORY

Stick designs made of kindergarten splints offer a means of developing the memory. The child watches the teacher or parent make a very simple design with two or three sticks. She may repeat the process two or three times. Then, the teacher's design being left on the table for the child to see, he is given the required number of sticks with which to copy the design.

If the child has difficulty, the adult might place one stick on the table, and have the child do the same; place another stick near the first, and have the child copy, and so on until the design is completed.

The very young child may not want to follow the example set by the adult. He may want to pile the sticks in a heap or line them up on the table. In this case, the adult might copy what the child has done, to help put across the idea of imitating.

If the child prefers to place the sticks in a row, the adult might use a number of red sticks for one row, blue ones for another row, and continue until the child remembers the order of colors. As the adult continues to accept the child's way of using the sticks, the child will gradually tend to reciprocate, and will eventually cooperate by following her way of using them.

Once the child has learned to copy some simple designs—squares, triangles, diamonds, houses, tables, chairs, and others—he may begin to construct designs from memory. The adult would make a design as the child watches, then remove the design, whereupon the child would try to remember how it was made and reconstruct it. In time, the child makes the transition from copying to *remembering*.

Objects may be used in memory exercises. Two or three objects may be placed in specific positions on a table—possibly one in each corner. The adult would remove them and put each back in the original position as the child watches. Then the objects would be removed from the table. Each object would be handed to the child who places it in the appropriate corner. Considerable practice may be required before the child masters this exercise. The number of objects and corresponding positions which would be included in the exercise will increase as the child's ability to remember develops.

Objects might be placed in various positions in a room as the child watches. Then they would be removed, and the child would put each back in its former place. This memory exercise may be combined with lipreading and speech preparation.

Objects might be placed about the room as the child watches. The adult would hold up a corresponding object and ask the child to find the other ball, airplane, etc. The child's memory in this instance would be measured by the speed and accuracy of response. Later, when the child has some grasp of lipreading, he would be asked to find the hidden objects without the aid of a corresponding object.

SENSE OF TOUCH

The geometric solids mentioned under *Shape* (page 99) are convenient in developing the sense of touch. The adult might place two or three of these solids in a paper bag while the child watches. She would pick up one of the corresponding shapes from the table, feel it, and then reach into the bag without looking into it, feel around, and pull out the solid that matches the one from the table.

The child would be given a solid to feel, then permitted to put his hand into the bag, feel the few solids in it until he touches the one which he thinks feels the same as the one on the table, and then pull it out.

The first shapes used in this way should be quite different in shape to facilitate the child's task of matching through touch alone. The number of shapes placed in the bag would be increased as the child's skill increases.

Toys may be placed in the "grab-bag" and used in a manner similar to that described above.

The cylinder board has been widely used in developing the sense of touch. After the child has mastered the matching of pegs to the corresponding holes in the cylinder board, he might be blindfolded and expected to do this from touch. Sometimes, it is necessary for the adult to perform this operation to show the child what is expected. Some children object to being blindfolded but will allow the adult to place her hands over their eyes. In the case of a child who objects strenuously to having his eyes covered, it would be advisable to eliminate the exercise until he is ready to accept it.

Children enjoy feeling materials and matching them. Two pieces of satin, two pieces of woolen fabric, two of cotton print, and other materials may be used. One set of fabrics might be sewn to a hoop or to a short stick to add interest. Some children enjoy having the materials pinned to a clothesline with clothespins. The child is given an opportunity to match the materials through *touch and sight*. When the child is able to match the materials in this way with ease, the exercise is made more exacting by introducing more colors and designs in the same materials. When the child has begun to show ability in matching materials through touch and sight, a few samples might be placed in a bag and chosen by touch only to match a particular material which the adult presents.

Children usually enjoy learning to match hard materials to hard ones, soft materials to other soft ones. Through feeling many objects and materials, the child learns that some are hard to the touch, some are soft, and he learns to group hard materials together, and soft materials together. Exercises with soft and hard materials offer practice in the lipreading of adjectives as well as in learning to identify materials through touch.

The importance of sense training in the early guidance of the deaf child has already been emphasized. It is advisable to combine lipreading, speech preparation, and auditory training with the sense training activities, but the parent and the teacher must be ever mindful that the value of the sense training activity can be nullified very easily by "improper" handling.

The activity, the child's effort and enjoyment, are more important than the adult's desire for responses in lipreading and speech. Through the use of sense training activities, the young deaf child may begin lipreading, and even imitation of speech, in a few weeks after the training is begun; or he may not show signs of lipreading nor any interest in imitating speech after months of sense training activities.

If measures are taken to force him to lipread before he is ready to do so, he will not only reject lipreading and its necessary allied activities, but will reject the sense training activity itself. These activities are extremely important in themselves, apart from lipreading and speech, and overanxiety by the parent or teacher for the development of those skills could retard the child in the development of sensory skills, which in turn retard the development of other skills that the deaf child needs.

The child must be given whatever time he requires to under-stand an activity, to complete it after he begins to understand, and to accept the idea of watching the speaker's face and lips as a part of the situation. It is not what the *adult* thinks the child *should do,* but what the *child needs* to do that is important.[19]

CHAPTER 11

Lipreading and Speech Activities
for Language Development

The activities described in this section are designed to build speech and lipreading vocabularies. The teacher and the parent consciously construct lessons around words that will be useful to the child in everyday life. Systematic planning is necessary in order that every lesson will have some value, even when changes "on the spot" become necessary to meet the needs of the individual child.

The person who is guiding the child will find that a small amount of specific training each day is more effective than a long period once or twice a week, especially in the case of the younger children—two- and three-year-olds.

Lipreading, speech, and auditory training are so closely combined that it would be difficult to say where one leaves off and the other begins. This is especially true of lipreading and speech with the very young child, and is the reason for presenting lipreading and speech activities as a unit in the pages that follow.

The adult will find that, as the child is exposed to more and more training, he reaches a stage where he is able to accept more intensified specific training. Then, adult and child may concentrate on either auditory training, lipreading, or speech preparation, to the exclusion of the others, for short periods. Throughout the preschool training, however, success in lipreading, in speech,

for young children

Specialized training is for mature clients.

104

in auditory training, will greatly depend on the degree to which the combined approach has been used.[147]

If the child is being trained to lipread a particular word, the adult would not only say that word as frequently as possible during the lesson, but would also grasp every opportunity to place the child's hand on her cheek as she says the word, would encourage the child to use his voice and to imitate, and would say the word near his ear or, if the situation permits the wearing of earphones, into a microphone.

multi-sensory approach

The parent or teacher of the young deaf child never endangers the potential success of a technique by sacrificing the child's comfort or mental health. Each child must be given time to adjust to any technique that might be introduced, and all lessons must be short. Five or ten minutes of keen enjoyment and interest produce better and longer-lasting results than half an hour of drudgery.

For purposes of discussion, the desirable exercises are grouped here under nouns, verbs, adjectives, etc. In practice, however, no one word is ever presented as a separate entity, but only as a word in relation to a real object, and to other words, so that whole phrases and sentences must necessarily enter each lesson.

Parent and teacher should become very familiar with the sense training exercises, as these overlap almost constantly the lipreading and speech preparation of the earlier stages.

THE PARTS OF SPEECH

NOUNS

The young deaf child's first introduction to lipreading generally comes through sense training exercises, primary of which are those connected with the matching of objects. Hence, the first words in lipreading are most naturally nouns—the names of these objects.

The teacher or the parent will find herself frequently reverting to these early matching exercises to facilitate the child's lipreading and speech training. As the child's interest in watching the lips and desire to understand through lipreading grow, he will become more and more independent of matching objects for purposes of lipreading.

But in the early lipreading and speech work, especially with the two- and three-year-olds, objects rather than pictures should be used, and only objects until the child has had an opportunity to make the transition from objects to pictures.

Parents have found that the children often want to pick the pictures from the pages or even to throw the pictures—reactions that are perfectly normal for the child who doesn't understand that the ball in the picture can't be picked up or thrown, as can the ball from the box of toys. But while objects are being used in the early specific lipreading and speech work, the object-picture relationship is being developed and clarified through sense training.

A group of three objects is sufficient for the first lessons, and the words would be those which do not look alike on the lips. *Car, ball,* and *airplane* might be the first words chosen for a lesson. After the child becomes familiar with the words, the one which he appears to lipread most easily might be omitted for a while and another object, such as a shoe, might be used with ball and airplane. At a later date, *car, shoe,* and *ball* might be used at one time; then *airplane, car,* and *shoe* in a group, and so on, in order that the number of words included in one lesson remains small. Variety is added to each lesson by making slight changes that do not cause confusion. Only one new word at a time is added to the familiar ones, providing for both challenge and success at once.

The adult would pick up each object and tell the child what it is as she holds his hand to her cheek. "This is a *ball.* This is a *car.* This is an *airplane.*" The ball might be given to the child and as his free hand is placed on the speaker's face, sentences such as, "You have the *ball,*" and "Put the *ball* into the box,"

Photo by Ross Madden   *Courtesy John Tracy Clinic*

PLATE VII.—Object held near speaker's face enables child to connect object and lip movements more easily.

Hands to own and others cheeks – Tadoma Method. (tactile).

Use new word often but in different constructions.

would be used. The child must be shown what is meant by putting the ball into the box. Whenever possible, the child's hand would be placed on his own cheek and he would be encouraged to imitate what the adult is saying.

A similar procedure is used when speaking of the other objects. Parent and teacher should not be afraid to talk about the objects in different ways. The same expressions need not be used time and again so long as the special words are repeated.[89] (Plate VII)

After the three objects have been put into the box, the adult might say, holding out her hand if necessary, "Find the *ball* and give it to me," or "Give me the *ball*. Yes, the *ball*."

The adult must be prepared for inaccurate responses, and be ready to help prevent the child's feeling insecure and inadequate in the situation. All too frequently, the little child's failure to produce the requested object results in the adult's using negative terms, such as *No,* with accompanying frowns, and it is not to be wondered at that the first word spoken by many deaf children is *No.* If the child picks up the car instead of the ball, the adult merely says, "That's a car. I want the ball." She replaces the car in the box, and asks again for the ball. When the right object is selected, it is not replaced in the box but is kept by the adult. If the child continues to have difficulty in spite of many repetitions of the spoken word, the adult might get another ball and say, "This is a *ball.* Now, give me the other ball."

When all three objects have been taken from the box, the adult might place them about the room—the ball in a corner, the car on the window sill, the airplane behind the door. As this is done, the child goes along and watches the adult as she speaks about each object. Child and adult return to their original positions and the adult asks for each object, using the tactile, visual, and auditory approaches. The child runs for each object and brings it back to the adult. Any failure on the part of the child should be treated very casually, and assistance be forthcoming.

Photo by Ross Madden   *Courtesy John Tracy Clinic*

PLATE VIII.—Use of the tactile (Tadoma) method by mother and child. (Tadoma method was developed by Miss S. Alcorn of the Detroit Day School for the Deaf.)

Paper bags may be used for further practice of these words. Three bags might be placed on the table along with the objects. The adult might say, "Show me the *ball*," and after the child indicates the ball—with or without help—the adult would open one bag, hold it before the child, and say, "Put the *ball* in the bag." The same procedure would be followed using *car* and *airplane*.

The adult would place the child's hand on her cheek, cover her mouth or place her hand over the child's eyes (if he will permit it), and say one of the words; for example, *"Car."* Immediately following this, the child would be permitted to see the speaker's lips as the word is repeated, and he would be shown that that object is in a certain bag. The same procedure follows for airplane and ball. The next time this operation is carried out, the child is given an opportunity to find the particular object by himself.

Over a period of time, the young child becomes relatively skillful at finding objects by the tactile means alone. Although he should be allowed to lipread along with the tactile means, he should also be given regular experience with "feeling speech," sometimes with lipreading and the auditory, sometimes without either lipreading or auditory. (Plate VIII)

Parent and teacher will find that the use of boxes and paper bags helps to maintain interest, especially in the case of the two- and three-year-olds who enjoy finding things, like to take objects out of things, or put them into something. One parent discovered that she got best results in lipreading and imitation of speech from her three-year-old when they sat on the floor by the bottom drawer of his bureau in the bedroom and hid toys under his clothing. Gradually, he became interested in working with the same objects in other situations, but his interest was first stimulated successfully through the child's desire to hide things in his drawer of clothing.

The three-year-old may enter into a number of activities re-

110

PLATE IX.—Speech play. Child learning to say "sh" as in shoe. Paper moves as breath is expelled. (See Bibliography, 146)

volving about a few objects in one lesson, without tiring and with interest, or he may remain attentive for just one activity. If his attention span is very short for such training, the lesson should be short and continued either later in the day or on the next day. <u>Teacher and parent are advised to have several sets of the objects, in different colors and sizes, so the child will feel a new interest, the while he is getting the necessary repetitive practice in the same words.</u>

The four-year-old who has had previous training for a year or two can be expected to do "more advanced" work with nouns. He may perform through lipreading many more actions involving objects and *pictures* of objects, and will use more speech as he imitates the adult.

Some four- and five-year-olds who have had earlier training enjoy working in groups of two or three, especially in playing "school," with one child as teacher and the rest as pupils. This situation has been especially successful with five-year-olds. The "teacher" asks a child for a specific object, another child for another object, etc.; and then another child takes a turn as "teacher." This exercise gives the children practice in lipreading one another, an experience which should begin at the preschool level.

lipreading among peers.

The child of four or five, depending on previous training and present skills, is likely to enjoy the following game. He is given a few picture cards; he and the adult review the names of them. Then the adult turns her back, the child says a word, and the teacher or parent turns around and indicates the corresponding picture. If the word is not said as well as the adult feels the child could say it, she pretends she does not understand, thus getting him to repeat it. This technique must be put over with discretion so that the child will not at any time feel that he is a failure, and that he cannot be understood.

The teacher and the parent construct lessons carefully around nouns that enable the child to become familiar with speech ele-

Photo by Ross Madden   Courtesy John Tracy Clinic

PLATE X.—Imitation of speech.

ments as they occur in whole words. There is no need for the use of printed forms to accomplish this. A small group of words, in which a specific sound is common to all, would be selected and used as were *airplane, car,* and *ball* in the previous examples of activities. (Plate IX)

Since *b* is easily seen on the lips, the words *boy, baby,* and *ball,* with corresponding objects or pictures, might constitute material for a series of lessons in lipreading and speech preparation. Such lessons tend to have more value over a period of time if auditory training is included in each one. It is emphatic that the child be *not* exposed to *b* or any other speech element alone, but only as it occurs in words. The element *b* alone means nothing to the child, and constant drill on the isolated form may result in the child's saying, "bu-aby," for "baby."

Other lessons may consist of words for practice in the use of *d,* such as *doll, daddy,* and *door;* of *fish, foot,* and *flower,* for practice in the use of *f;* and so on. As the child's experience, training, and total readiness develop, the words in the lipreading lessons may be grouped according to the initial consonant, so that words beginning with *p* would be used in one lesson or in one part of a lesson, those beginning with *th* in another, and so on. Later, words which end in the same consonant might be grouped together, and those with a common central consonant together; for example, *drum* and *gum* might be used in the same lesson, *paper* and *supper* in another.

It must be kept in mind that, although such groupings are designed to familiarize the young child with specific speech elements, he cannot at once imitate them. The child needs considerable practice in seeing them on the lips as they occur in whole words before he should be expected to try them himself. The daily lipreading practice in relation to interesting objects and activities gradually impresses him with the formation of those sounds; and little by little he learns to recognize similarities and differences in the sounds and to imitate them with increasing success, as he tries out a whole word, or as much of each word as he is able to manage. (Plate X)

As the child's ability to lipread nouns progresses, those nouns should be grouped not only according to initial, medial, and final consonants, but may also be grouped according to such classifications as food, furniture, toys, transportation, animals, dishes, things outdoors, clothing, parts of the body, family, friends, etc. In time, the nouns which he must learn for lipreading and speech are included in charts of many varieties which add interest to the training he must have.

A wealth of materials is necessary to this preparatory speech and lipreading training, and the parent and teacher find that many individual pictures, individual table-size charts, and larger wall charts must be prepared, to keep the child interested and to provide acceptably for the repetition he requires.

pictures, charts, books, diagrams

One need not be an artist to make attractive speech and lipreading cards, charts, and books. There is no point in spending hours laboriously coloring outline pictures when they may be cut out quickly from current magazines. When a required picture is not immediately available in a magazine or picture book, the parent and teacher may find it necessary to draw and color one; but this occasional necessity need not be made a grueling task.

Each word to which the child is exposed for lipreading and speech preparation should be illustrated on its own separate card. Each child should have small charts which fit easily on his table or desk and which he can manipulate with ease. There should also be larger charts which can be hung on the wall or stood on the floor. The child also enjoys having his own book of words he has learned to lipread, and of words he can say with some intelligibility.

The parent and the teacher are advised against putting too many pictures on one page or one chart. It is more effective to have three charts for food, where the pictures are clear-cut and

115

FIG. 1.—Suggested charts for lipreading; others for animals, clothing, people, parts of the body, etc. Mounted or drawn. The five-year-old could use these charts with the printed word beside each picture.

well-spaced, than to have all the pictures of the food on one chart and so closely spaced that the child has difficulty in recognizing any one picture quickly.

Figure 1 shows examples of charts or pages in the individual child's book which may be used for lipreading practice of nouns. As the child's vocabulary grows, he may make one little book of toys, another of food, etc.

Figures 2 and 3 show charts which may be used in familiarizing the child with speech elements.

In the training situations, the large chart may be used one day, the table-size chart on another day, and the child's individual book or books on another; and there may be situations when a combination of these may be used.

When the child is learning to indicate certain objects through lipreading, he might be given a little wooden pointer with which to indicate the specific words on the larger charts. Using such a gadget or plaything makes the process somewhat more acceptable to the child.

The small charts are useful in auditory training along with lipreading and speech preparation since they require less table-space than a series of single cards or the larger chart. The child lipreads the adult, points to the picture on the chart, imitates the word as he places one hand on the speaker's face and one on his own cheek, and listens to the adult's and then to his own voice as each speaks into the microphone of the hearing aid. Later, the earphones may be removed, and as each object is spoken of by the adult, the child would find it on his small chart and also on the larger wall chart.

Four- and five-year-olds with some previous training and progress in language understanding through lipreading, will find printed words appearing beside or below the pictures in their speech and lipreading books and on the charts. The same charts or similar ones may be used with five-year-olds in lessons that

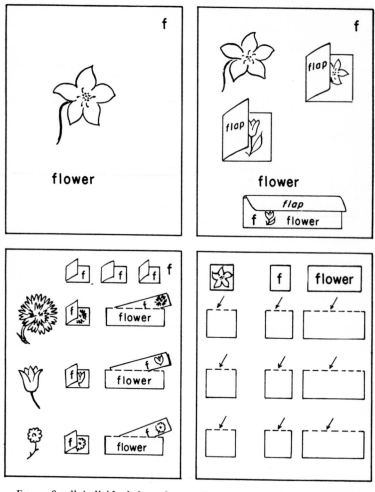

Fig. 2.—Small, individual charts for speech and lipreading and auditory training for four- and five-year-olds. Same ideas omitting the printed forms are excellent for three-year-olds, and some two- and two-and-a-half-year-olds.

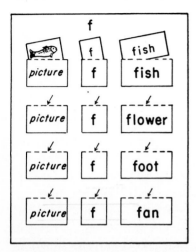

Column 1: Picture of object beginning with *f* sound would be pasted on outside of pocket—child inserts matching picture after lipreading it and saying it. *Column 2:* Sound is printed on outside of pocket for four- and five-year-olds. Child says sound, finds corresponding card on table and inserts opposite word he has used in column one. *Column 3:* Printed word is placed on outside of pocket for five-year-olds; child finds corresponding flash card on table, says the word, and inserts card in pocket.

FIG. 3.—A chart made of cardboard on which paper pockets or envelopes are pasted serve as interesting practice material for lipreading, imitation of speech, spontaneous speech, and may be used with ease in auditory training. Similar charts may be made for each vowel and consonant. The sections involving printed forms would not be applicable to three-year-olds or younger. Printed forms may be included with four- and five-year-olds, as long as interest is centered in speech and lipreading, and emphasis is *not* placed on the printed words.

combine lipreading, speech, and word matching. Figure 4 shows charts that may be used for such purposes.

Teacher and parent will find envelopes very useful in adding variety to the lessons. These envelopes may be kept separate or they may be pasted, flap-side out, to large pieces of cardboard. One envelope may be used as a container for pictures of toys, another for pictures of clothing; or each envelope might contain pictures of objects whose names begin with a common sound. Each time a child finds a picture from lipreading, he may say the word, and place the picture in the envelope. Any procedure that includes some action on the part of the child seems to be more effective than mere lipreading and speech with the same words in the same way, day in and day out.

The blackboard, cut-outs of paper or felt, hand puppets,[22] black silhouettes of objects, lotto games, dolls,[18] peep-shows, and other such devices help to make the lessons more enjoyable for adult and child.

Objects may be traced on felt and the design cut out. Then, as the child lipreads and says each word, the corresponding object may be placed on its slightly larger piece of felt, to which it will stick without pasting. This process seems to fascinate every child.

Hand puppets and paper dolls are very helpful in learning the names of clothing and parts of the body. Dolls are sometimes useful in encouraging children to place the hand on the speaker's face, and many a deaf child has played at "talking" to her doll, placing the doll's hand on her own cheek. Surprise situations, games, color, variety, mystery, etc., all aid in developing attention span, deeper interest, better cooperation and understanding.

Colorful classrooms and training areas, where pictures and objects, well-chosen to be within the range and interest of each child, are tastefully arranged, are themselves stimulating. Nothing can be more boring and uninviting than a bare room where lipreading and speech are carried on over a little table, with mere routine talking by the adult and parroting by the child. The imaginative, ingenious, interested, and courageous adult, whether teacher or parent, finds no more satisfaction under those conditions than does the child.

The young child, who, in the middle of a lesson, will pull off the earphones, run to a shelf for a picture or to a book or chart to find a picture or object that is related to the lesson, is a much happier and more interested child than the one who just sits and does "as he is told" day after day, month in and month out, in fear of moving. The adult may be reasonably certain that such a child is escaping from the situation in some way, if only in imagination; and everything possible must be done to prevent this. Deviation from the planned lesson often promotes

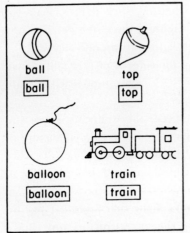

FIG. 4.—Suggested charts for combining lipreading, speech and word matching. The words in the squares represent separate strips of paper or cardboard on which the word is printed. These charts might be made about note-book size, so that each child could have a set. Larger wall charts of the same type are effective for five-year-olds in group teaching.

lipreading and speech, and will certainly produce a much healthier situation than one in which the child must find relief in his own imaginary situations.[47]

VERBS

Action verbs such as *bow, run, fall, jump, walk*, etc., are used in the first lipreading and speech lessons on verbs. As in the case of nouns, many charts and pictures are required. The teacher and the parent will have on hand a collection of separate pictures of each verb. Charts needed for the study of each verb are very easily made. The *run* chart would include pictures of a dog running, a man running, a girl running, a cat running, and a boy running. This type of chart helps to put across the idea that the action of running may be performed by different people and animals, and also gives practice in the use of nouns with the verb.

levels of symbolization Pictures in silhouette cut from black paper may be used as well as colored, more detailed pictures. Stick figures, made of straight lines, may also be used. Figure 5 shows the detailed picture, the silhouette, and the stick figure, all on one chart.

The young child enjoys finding the colored picture and matching it to the silhouette and the stick figure, and each picture offers an opportunity for using speech.

If the verb *bow* is being practiced, the following procedure might be used. The teacher shows the child a colored picture of a girl bowing and says, "The girl is *bow*ing. I can *bow*." Teacher bows. "You bow, Jean. *Bow*." Child bows. "I bowed and you bowed."

The child is asked to find on one of the charts another picture of a girl bowing. After indicating the correct picture, the child's hand is placed on the adult's cheek and the child is encouraged to speak with the adult and to imitate afterwards, "The girl is bowing," and "Bow." The child is given practice in clapping for accent as the sentence is used.

FIG. 5.—Verb chart.

The child might be asked to bow again, and then assisted in saying, "I bowed."

This work with action verbs must involve variety and activity. A child can become so weary of bowing and hopping day after day, in the same place and for no apparent reason, that the practice can lose all its value.

Four- and five-year-olds who have had an early start in this work often enjoy practicing action verbs in small groups where they have an opportunity of telling one another what action to perform. The adult who is doing the guiding must not only provide opportunity for lipreading these verbs but for the use of them by the child, both separately and in short sentences. This frequently requires the adult's acting as the pupil while the child plays teacher, especially where group work is not yet possible.

Additional verbs are introduced into the lessons as the child's age and learning capacity permit. The verbs would be those which arise in conversational situations, which will occur later in reading readiness books, and which may be illustrated; for example, *laugh, cry, buy, give, dig, make, draw, paste, cut, eat, sleep,* and others.

Children at the nursery and kindergarten levels enjoy owning their own series of little verb books. These are easily made by the parent and teacher. One book might consist of many pictures illustrating the verb *run,* another for *walk,* until the child has a book for each verb learned for lipreading.

Each child might also have a book of verbs which he has learned to use in speaking. One page in this speech book might illustrate a few verbs which begin with *p,* such as *pull, push,* and *play.* Another page might illustrate the verbs, *burn, buy,* and *bow.* These speech books may be used in some of the lessons as another way of practice in saying the verbs, using the tactile, visual, and auditory techniques. The single verb would be spoken as well as whole sentences using the verb. For example, the child should have practice in using *sleep:* "The boy is sleeping," "I slept"; *run:* "The dog is running," "I ran"; and others, in appropriate situations.

There has been some question regarding the advisability of using verbs in the present progressive form with young deaf children; and yet the parents are strongly advised to talk to the child as they would to a hearing child. If a hearing child sees another child running and if he were to comment on what he sees, he would say, "Bobby's running," since that is the form he has heard from the adults in his environment. The very young hearing child might say just "Run," and the adult would probably follow this up with, "Yes, Bobby's running." The deaf child must have the opportunity of becoming conscious of the various forms in which a verb may be used, even though he is not yet able to use the right form for every situation.[2]

Five-year-olds who will work in small groups, and occasionally two or three four-year-olds who have had previous training and who will work together in a group for a very short period, may enjoy the following verb game. The adult might say to one child, "Billy, let me see you *walk*." While Billy walks, the adult says to the other children, "Billy is walking." When Billy comes back and sits down, the teacher or parent goes to him, places his hand on her cheek and says, pointing to him, using his finger to point to himself, and encouraging him to imitate, "I walked." Then she might point to herself and each other child in turn, and say, "I didn't walk, Jimmy didn't walk, Doris didn't walk, *Billy walked*." Then each of the other children would be assisted in saying, "Billy walked."

[handwritten margin note: putting verb across in group therapy]

Each of the other children would be given an opportunity to participate by acting out the same or another verb, and of using it as well as he is able, and the appropriate form would be used by the adult.

Exercises of this type where "correct"—that is, normal—verb forms are used, help to lay the foundation for future language work involving tenses. Certainly the child will not be expected to use all the tenses of verbs, to which he has been exposed at the preschool level, on his entrance to Grade I. He would be a very exceptional deaf child if he did. The most that can be expected is that he will be aware to some degree of different ways of saying things at certain times, of an action taking place here and now, of an action that has been completed, and of an action that may take place later on.

Even after he has entered Grade I and has had further specific training, he will probably need prompting by the teacher and the parent. However, an early experience of this sort with verbs should help him to cope with tenses in the grades; to get the meaning of a statement where the particular tense has significance; and to feel secure since this language is not entirely unfamiliar to him. Impressions received, even unconsciously, while the child is still at the most impressionable stages definitely increase his ability to recall related experiences and use them to interpret new ones.

Games that revolve about the store, the post office, the play-house, the farm, the zoo, the beach, etc., are easily improvised by the adult and interesting to the child, and are helpful in verb study. Make-believe situations should be similar to real ones which the child has experienced. For example, the play-store situation will mean much more to the child in every respect if he has had experience in going to the store with his mother.

Empty wooden crates provide shelf and counter space for play-store activities. Canned goods, empty cartons, and paper boxes with the original pictures on them serve as materials to be purchased. Paper money may be used, although many children like to pretend that they are handling money without using either the real or substitute variety. (Plate XI)

The child should get practice in using such expressions as, "Milk, please," "Thank you," "I bought some milk."

Activities throughout the day provide for practice in lipreading such commands as, "Close the door," "Bring me the ball," "Open the door," "Give Betty the flower," etc. Occasionally they may be included in a lesson. However, unless they can be incorporated into the lesson in interesting, meaningful ways, it is advisable to spend very little time in specific situations in the lipreading of such expressions. They are, of course, important; but unless the adult uses discretion in presenting them, the situations may become boring and superficial.

Printed forms of the verbs begin to appear below the illustrations of verbs when the child is at the four-year-old level, and the single verbs and sentences with the verbs *may appear* with illustrations when the child is at the five-year level. Please note that these words only *appear,* since the printed form is not stressed at this time. The child at the preschool level must become familiar with printed forms, although understanding the verbs and learning to use them in speaking *must* come first. Placing stress on the printed form of the verb, prematurely, can retard the understanding and use of it in speech, since the preschool years are not long enough for everything. If wisely used,

126

Photo by Ross Madden   *Courtesy John Tracy Clinic*

PLATE XI.—Play-store for lipreading and speech practice.

the printed word may add to the child's language experiences even at this level.

Each time that the printed word or sentence is attached correctly to the illustration of a specific verb, the child is being given another opportunity to lipread and to talk.

to have
to be

Parents and teachers have found that forms of *to have* and *to be* frequently present problems for the child. Needless to say, it would be quite impossible to "teach" the preschool deaf child the many forms of these verbs, and it would be very foolish to attempt to do so. He should get practice, however, in lipreading and using some of the simpler forms.

The deaf child confuses the two verbs, sometimes until he is well on in the grades, and he has been heard saying, "I have tall," instead of, "I am tall." This confusion certainly is understandable. Hearing children have difficulty at times in achieving the correct uses. Some early work in this for the deaf child can facilitate later work.

The young child's growing consciousness of possessions and his desire to possess his own property provide for practice of *I have.* The young child should be exposed to, and be encouraged to imitate, such sentences as, "I have a ball," "Mother has a hat," "The boy has a rabbit," etc., in situations which lend themselves naturally to such expressions. Later on, when the child has become more interested in spoken language and aware of the relationship between *have* or *has* and possession, he should have a collection of pictures illustrating, "A boy *has* a wagon," "A girl *has* a doll," "A man *has* a car," etc., and he should be encouraged to say the whole sentence with the adult. His own possessions might be grouped together for some lessons, in which such sentences as, "I *have* a gun," I *have* a wagon," "I *have* a doll," would be used.

Four- and five-year-olds should have practice in using such sentences as, "I *am* Bob," "I *am* a boy," etc. *I am* and *I'm* should be alternated, since both are commonly used in conversational language.

A great deal may be done at the preschool level to establish the understanding and use of *have* and *has.*

Less, specifically speaking, can be done in the case of *to be,* because of the abstract nature of its forms, *is, am,* etc. However, the adult should take every opportunity to use the various forms, and, as the child nears the five- and six-year levels, some effort may be made to render him more aware of what the adult says, without requiring him to use the various forms correctly himself. When he is looking at books with pictures of boys, girls, men, and women, the adult calls his attention to the fact that, "This is John," "I am not John," "I am Mother," or "I am Miss———," "You are Bobby," etc. Then the adult might ask the child, "Are you John?" and assist the child in answering, "No; I am Bobby." Such incidents may be brief and casual, but they are important.

In all the work with verbs, the "correct" forms of each must be used in relation to activities that are meaningful to the child and enjoyable. Drills that are exacting and often meaningless to the child are not advisable, and are not necessary in building the kind of foundation most essential to future language skills.

ADJECTIVES

The young child's interest in *things* provides many opportunities for practice in learning to lipread and use adjectives. When the child sees an object, he usually has some feeling about it. He may be attracted or repelled by its color, its size, its shape, the use to which it may be put, or some other characteristic. The characteristics of each object may be described by the use of adjectives together with familiar nouns and verbs.

The child should be exposed to the many adjectives which would be used day after day in describing objects that enter into the child's experiences. However, in the specific lesson situations, it is advisable to work within a limited sphere, giving the child a great deal of repetition in the use of very few adjectives until they are fairly well-established.

Color—Adjectives

Colors attract most children, but their names may or may not be easy for the children to lipread. Teacher and parent must be ready to accept this situation if it arises. Too often, young deaf children have been expected to learn to lipread colors easily, just because of their apparent interest in colors.

The child has already had some experience with matching colors in his sense training activities, and probably has made a start in lipreading a few color-names at that time. He has probably learned to recognize similarities and differences in colors.

The first colors chosen for lipreading would depend somewhat on the child's preferences but more upon which color-names look different in speech. *Blue* and *yellow* might be the first ones chosen.

Since only two colors are to be used in the first lessons for specific lipreading and speech, several objects of each of these colors are needed to hold the child's interest. The same blue object and the same yellow one, day after day, may lose all attraction for the child and such a situation would certainly do little to broaden his concept of the colors and the words.

Although colors are used in phrases and sentences in real situations throughout each day, the specific lessons on color adjectives for the first few weeks, possibly months, would be concerned with individual words. This does *not* imply that the single word is repeated over and over, apart from other words; but that the color, itself, is to be emphasized. For example, if a series of blue and yellow objects were being used, the adult would indicate the yellow ball and say, "That's a *yellow* ball. It's yellow." Then, indicating other objects, she would say, "That's *yellow*, that's *yellow,* and that's *yellow.*" A similar procedure would apply to the blue objects.

Then, all objects, except one blue and one yellow, would be removed from the immediate area, and put in various places about the room. The adult would point to the yellow object near by, place the child's hand on her cheek and say, "That's *yellow.* It's *yellow.*" The child's other hand would be placed on his own cheek and he would be encouraged to repeat, both with and without the adult's assistance, "That's yellow," or "Yellow." The blue object would be used in a similar manner.

Practice would follow in lipreading the two color words, as the adult says, "Show me the *yellow* ball," and "Which is the *blue* ball?" Then looking about the room, she might say, "Find me something else that is *yellow.*" "Find something *blue,*" etc., until all the blue and yellow objects have been collected.

Day after day, for short periods, these color words would be practiced, using tactile, visual, and auditory means in connection with many objects, pictures, charts, and activities, until the child shows some indication of understanding through lipreading what is meant by *blue* and *yellow.*

The next lessons might consist of *red* and *yellow,* then *red* and *blue,* then *purple* and *yellow,* and occasionally three colors may be included in one lesson as the child becomes more adept at lipreading. The adult must not make the error of hurrying the child, of expecting him to learn to lipread all the color names within a few months, or even in a whole year, of training.

The *color phrase* composed of a color adjective and a noun has been presented to the child in many situations before specific work in this area is begun. His readiness for it will depend largely on his general language understanding, and ability to lipread isolated nouns and color adjectives. Some three-year-olds have been able to start this work; other children aren't ready until they are four or even five years old.

When specific lipreading and speech revolving about the color

131

phrase are begun, it is wise to use in each lesson a series of phrases in which there is a constant, familiar word. For example, a lesson might include a group of phrases such as, *a red shoe, a red ball, a red house,* and *a red car.* Another group of phrases for a lesson might include *a blue shoe, a blue ball, a blue house, a blue car.* For variation, a group of phrases such as, *a yellow shoe, a red shoe, a blue shoe,* and *a pink shoe,* might be practiced. The use of a constant color throughout, *or* of a constant noun with different colors, provides the gradual building up of a vocabulary which so many deaf children need.

After the child has had a wealth of experiences in lipreading and saying such phrases, the exercises might be made considerably more difficult and challenging by including in one lesson separate phrases; as, *a red ball, a blue cup, a yellow hat,* etc. This demands more concentration on the part of the child.

The child who finds color less interesting, and who learns very slowly to lipread the colors, must be approached very patiently, and the lessons for him should be made especially interesting and appealing. The fact that he doesn't lipread the colors easily is no indication that he is not capable of eventually doing so, nor that he is retarded. One child may lipread colors, separately and in phrases at the three-year-old level, while another child who is quite as intelligent may need all the preschool years or even longer to accomplish the same end.

As the child learns to lipread each color, it would be illustrated in his little book designed for this purpose; and the colors which he learns to say with some intelligibility would be illustrated in his speech book of colors.

The printed form of each color name and each color phrase may be included when the child is ready for that. As in the case of other printed forms already discussed, the emphasis would be on understanding and speech preparation, rather than on the printed form.

Photo by Ross Madden   *Courtesy John Tracy Clinic*

PLATE XII.—Father records and participates in speech and lip-reading lesson revolving about number work.

Number—Adjectives

The child's first specific experience with numbers usually comes through sense training exercises when he learns to match cards illustrating a certain number of circles, squares, and other number pictures.

The child will not learn to lipread the numbers as quickly as he will learn to match the cards illustrating the number pictures; and this fact necessitates the use of many sets of number cards to provide interest and the required amount of repetition. Each time a number picture is presented, and the child matches it to another on charts and in number books, the adult talks about it. "That's *one,* that's *one,* and that's *one.*"

It takes time for the child to realize that two spots are equal in number to two shoes, and that two blue circles are equal in number to two green circles. Each difference in color and shape that enters into the number work presents another transition which the young child must make. For this reason, parents are particularly cautioned against moving ahead faster than the child is able to assimilate numbers.

The first number cards should be simple and identical. After the child learns to match one blue circle to one blue circle, he learns to match one blue to one green, two blue to two purple, two chairs to two chairs, two chairs to two tables, etc., and finally reaches the stage where he can place all number pictures of two together, all ones together, all threes together, regardless of whether the pictures show squares, circles, chairs, balls, or any other objects. Throughout this number experience, the tactile, visual, and auditory means are used to promote lipreading and speech. (Plate XII)

Number charts similar to those in Figures 6 and 7 add interest to the child's daily training in number work. Number books also provide for greater interest and further practice.

Besides learning to recognize number pictures, the child should

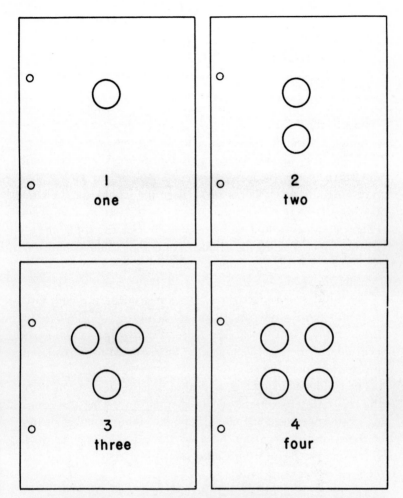

FIG. 6.—Suggested number cards, or pages in scrapbook, for the five-year-old. Similar cards to five or six. Additional cards illustrating cars, airplanes, apples, etc., would be used. These might also be used for word matching. Number symbols and words are added as the child's age and responses indicate a readiness.

have some experience in learning to count. The events of each day usually provide some opportunity for counting; and once the child begins to count, he is often found counting his possessions for others, counting the blocks he plays with, and so on, even before he is able to count very far or to say the numbers intelligibly.

The teacher and the parent use a number of simple exercises, similar to the following one, to give the child a broader concept of numbers through counting. The adult might take a number of blocks from a shelf where many blocks are kept. She would take three blocks and place them in a row on the table. Then indicating the other blocks in her lap, she would ask the child for "three" more blocks, and would help him to find them. Then one block would be placed on each of the three already on the table. Taking the child's hand, she would count, *one, two, three,* moving the child's hand from block to block and from left to right.

The adult might place three blocks in front of her, and three in front of the child, and both adult and child would count (from left to right) *one, two, three.* The rhythm of the movement and of the speech should not be sacrificed for articulation during this operation.

The child should get a great deal of practice in counting many objects, from left to right and in rhythm. Following this counting experience, the adult might show the child a number picture of three, and demonstrate how the three blocks may be made into a number picture. This often means placing a block on each pictured object on the card.

The recognition of number pictures should be correlated with counting as often as possible. But it must be clearly understood by the adult doing the guiding that the child should be trained to recognize the number picture as whole, and *not* have to *count* the objects in the constructed picture.

Counting is important, and usually of interest to the child;

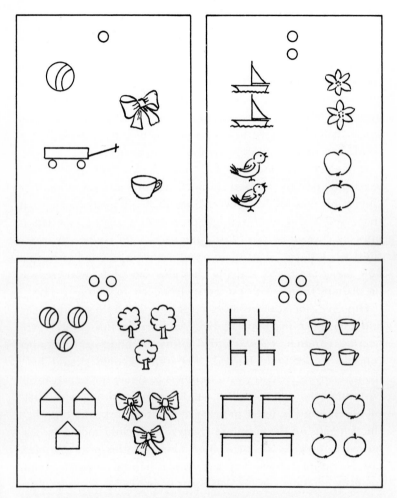

FIG. 7.—Suggested number charts for lipreading and speech. Child learns to recognize immediately the number picture without counting. Large wall charts and smaller individual ones make this number work more effective.

but it is not as simple as many adults seem to believe. The child may repeat numbers after the adult, and "count" just as far as he is "trained" to count, but this is no indication that the child has a well-rounded concept of each number named. It is far more important to the child that he have a well-rounded concept of each number, from one to five or six, by the time he enters Grade I, than that he be able to "count" to twenty, or even to a hundred, if he does not realize that *five* is more than *three,* that *five* may be in the form of a picture, a symbol, or a word; and that *five* may mean five chairs in his home.

It has been mentioned several times already that the preschool years provide time for just so much training and no more. The child can't possibly learn everything about numbers during that time; and the person training the child—a parent especially—must be content to put "first things first." Of course, there are times when the child wants to count many objects and to be told how many are there, and his questions should be answered, as he perhaps counts with the adult from left to right.

However, the teacher must recognize the child's immaturity and remember that, on the basis of work in this subject with hearing children, every child's ability to understand number concepts is definitely limited. The three-year-old should have many, many experiences with numbers to three; the four-year-old with numbers to four, and so on. Thorough training with a few numbers results in faster progress in number work later on, when the demands on the child are greater. Each child should be permitted to progress as fast as he is able; but this principle must not be misinterpreted nor the child's natural curiosity about quantity exploited, to the detriment of present and future training.

The enriched number program within the child's comprehension may seem not too interesting to the adult and will surely involve a maximum of ingenuity and imagination on his part; but it is the only kind of program that the child should have.

The procedure in presenting number phrases is similar to that described for color phrases. Although numbers should be used in phrases and sentences as much as possible, specific work with them must be gradual and well-planned for the individual child.

Number work is usually fun for the young child. It lends itself easily to many activities, such as hiding and finding, and other game-like situations. The child gets practice in lipreading the numbers in phrases, sentences, and stories as well as separately, and in using the numbers in speaking and in answering questions.

The question form *How many* is used over and over in many situations of an adequate early training program, so that, by the time the child enters Grade I, he should seldom make an error in answering a simple question of *How many*. But even a very intelligent child will not be able to acquire this power if precious time has been devoted to "teaching" him to count or to understand number concepts far beyond his capacity to grasp.

OTHER ADJECTIVES

The deaf child of three to five or six years of age may learn to lipread, and in some degree to say, such adjectives as *big* and *small* (or *little*), *soft* and *hard*, *pretty* and *funny*, *old* and *new*, *good* and *bad*, etc. Descriptive adjectives like these are used frequently in most environments and the parent should try to show the child through the use of pictures, objects, and real situations, what is meant by each. When the child is ready for specific work involving these adjectives, he seems to learn to lipread and use them most easily when they are presented in the comparative sense; for example, the *big* ball stands out because the one beside it is *small*. The obvious differences help to explain the adjectives.

The first work is in relation to matching objects and matching pictures illustrating such adjectives. Many pictures and charts are necessary for lipreading and speech practice, even long after the child has become less dependent on object matching and picture matching.

These adjectives would be used separately, in phrases, and in sentences, and the child would be encouraged to use them in the lesson situations and in spontaneous speech.

PREPOSITIONS

During the first year in nursery school, if the child is three years of age or under, no specific work is done with prepositions. The child will have some *incidental* experience with prepositions at these early levels in relation to the work with nouns and verbs and in daily conversational situations. For example, when the child is asked to find a ball and put it *in* a box or *on* the table, when he is told to put his coat *in* the locker, and to carry out other requests, he is inevitably getting some valuable experience in the use of prepositions.

When the adult says, "The ball is on the chair," the child eventually realizes that there is some connection between *ball* and *chair,* and even though he may be quite unaware of the word *on,* his understanding of the whole sentence is a very real achievement that will make special work with prepositions more meaningful for him later.

Some four-year-olds and most five-year-olds may begin specific work on prepositions. The amount and nature of such training will depend on the individual child and his general language background. It would be an error to impose such training upon the child who has not some understanding of language through lipreading and who hasn't established some lipreading and speech vocabulary. And, under no conditions, would any child at the preschool level be exposed to a purely technical consideration of the use of prepositions.

In so far as any preschool deaf child is able to understand any preposition, he will achieve that understanding through activities related to familiar words such as nouns and verbs.

Two prepositions such as *under* and *on*, which are easily illustrated and which do not look alike on the lips, might be used in the first lessons. The child might be given a number of objects and asked to put one *on* the table, another *under* the table, another *on* the table, another *under* the table, etc. Preposition charts that illustrate the objects (which correspond to the real ones) *on* and *under* tables might be used in connection with the game.

Figure 8 shows samples of charts which may be made for each preposition. In the charts is set forth a carefully devised sequence to be followed in simplifying for the child his understanding of the preposition through lipreading.

Preposition books are helpful and of interest to the child. He might have an *On* book consisting of many pictures of familiar objects *on* many familiar objects; another book for *Under,* etc.

The child is encouraged to imitate the whole phrase or sentence in which the particular preposition is used. In order to make it clearer to the child, the adult may stress the preposition without breaking the rhythm of the sentence; for example, "The ball is *on* the box," "The ball is *on* the floor," "The ball is *on* the table."

In spontaneous speech situations, most preschool deaf children will eliminate the preposition, and will continue to do so long after they have learned to understand it in sentences, and even to use it in the specific speech situations where they are prompted by the adult. In spite of all the excellent early training the child may have, he will probably have to be prompted more often than not, after entering Grade I.

The five-year-old who has had two or three years of previous language training may be reminded casually of his omission, and assisted in repeating the sentence using the preposition. These casual reminders, in addition to such specific exercises as those

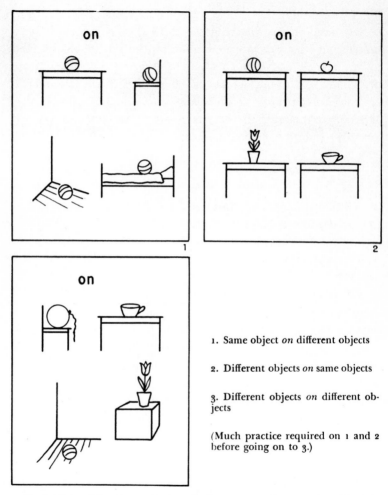

1. Same object *on* different objects

2. Different objects *on* same objects

3. Different objects *on* different objects

(Much practice required on 1 and 2 before going on to 3.)

FIG. 8.—Preposition charts. Pictures may be cut out and mounted, or drawn in outline and colored. Similar series for each preposition. Large wall charts of each type supplemented by individual ones for each child.

described above, constitute the extent to which the child may be trained in the understanding and use of prepositions. As a preschool child, he is not ready for a more analytical approach to language, and if at the end of his preschool training he has acquired a relatively broad understanding of two or three prepositions, he will have done well indeed.

PRONOUNS

The little deaf child should have been exposed to pronouns in simple language from the time people began to talk to him. In spite of this exposure in earlier stages, the three-year-old shows little if any understanding of any pronoun. As the child continues through the preschool years, his attention may be called to such pronouns as *I, me, you,* and *mine,* as they occur in sentences and other expressions. These pronouns may be more emphasized in working with the four-year-old, although he would not be expected to use them. In the lesson situation he might be encouraged to say, "I have a gun," instead of merely saying, "Gun." The adult responds with, "Yes, *you* have a gun. *I* have no gun."

When the child finally becomes conscious of these words he is often confused by the way *you* and *I* are used. He can't quite accept *you* calling him *you,* when he is supposed to refer to himself as *I*. And when he realizes that *I, me,* and *mine,* may all be used in relation to himself, he may use any one of them to the exclusion of others or may use all of them, usually in the "wrong" situation. However, he is using them; and with each occasion when he is reminded casually of the "correct" form, the confusion gradually passes and, sooner or later, the pronouns fall into place.

For the most part, right up to the end of the preschool training, the best practice in the use of pronouns is provided by general conversation. The specific work helps to make the child more conscious of pronouns and their respective meanings, but it is the casual practice that he gets from day to day which counts the most in the end. It is very difficult for either parent or teacher to determine what pronouns the child actually "knows," but they can be certain that constant exposure to pronouns during the preschool years, no matter what confusion the child may exhibit, will make his future language work much more meaningful and less difficult to master.

From the lipreader's standpoint, pronouns can be very elusive. While trying to understand the connected language of a speaker, many a child, or adult, will miss the whole sense of a remark through a misinterpretation of a pronoun. The parent and the teacher can help the child to obviate many difficult situations in the future by establishing some early foundation for understanding pronouns.[78]

CONJUNCTIONS

Conjunctions, like any other commonly used language form, occur very early in the child's general language training. The specific training, however, cannot be begun until the child's general language understanding, his vocabulary, and his attention span indicate his readiness. For example, a three-year-old who has learned to lipread the words *ball* and *shoe,* and who is asked to find the ball *and* the shoe, may dash off to get the ball without watching the speaker until she has completed the request.

When the child is ready to watch for longer spoken phrases and sentences, he usually enjoys being able to find more than one object, or performing more than one action, as would be required in exemplifying the conjunction *and.* Four-year-olds, after the necessary preparatory language training, are able to lipread such expressions as, "Show me a ball *and* an airplane." "A car *and* a truck," "A girl *and* a boy," etc. The five-year-old takes another step forward when he learns to lipread, "Show me a ball, a car, *and* an airplane."

Four- and five-year-olds learn to lipread and carry out such commands as, "Run *and* fall," "Walk to the door, turn around, *and* run to me," "Find the picture of the girl sleeping *and* the picture of the boy running," etc.

Attention is brought to the conjunction as the speaker uses the tactile, visual, and auditory techniques, and the child is encouraged to imitate the whole expression.

In the formal lesson, the child learns to use the word *and,* although in spontaneous speech situations he tends to omit it. At the five-year-old level, he may be reminded of his omission and encouraged to repeat the expression in full.

The conjunction *or* figures in daily situations in expressions such as, "Which do you want, the red socks *or* the blue ones?" "Do you want the wagon *or* the truck?" For some time, when the adult asks, "Do you want the red ball *or* the blue one?" the child, in all probability, will reach for both balls. Only constant practice in making choices, an experience which is often difficult and frustrating for the young child, can establish any concept of the conjunction *or,* and in spite of the maximum practice possible during the preschool years, the deaf child at the end of that time has little real understanding of *or.*

The conjunction *and* should be fairly well established at the end of the preschool training, and other conjunctions such as *or,* although not established to any noticeable degree, should have become a regular part of the language experiences.

PHRASES AND SENTENCES

Phrases have been mentioned several times in relation to adjectives, prepositions, and conjunctions. It is important that the child be exposed to the use of phrases from the beginning of his training. Gradually he is trained to lipread and to say simple phrases made up of familiar words he has learned.

The last year of preschool training should include some daily work in lipreading phrases, in saying them, and in listening to them. Any work with the printed forms must be done in conjunction with lipreading, speech, and auditory training.

Granted that the child has had the necessary preparatory training, he usually is able, by the time he enters Grade I, to lipread with relative ease such common phrases as *two cars, three big boys, a blue balloon, a pretty dress,* and others, using the colors, the numbers, and other adjectives with familiar nouns.

The child is also able to use some phrases in answering questions; for example, "Where is the basket?" *"On the table."* "Where did you go yesterday?" *"Down town."*

His speech may be quite intelligible, or it may be almost unintelligible. It is hoped that the child's speech will be sufficiently intelligible for the listener to distinguish what he means to say, since the most important accomplishment of the whole preschool time is that the child understand spoken language and begin to try to use the same language.[85]

Sentences are used in talking to the child throughout his early training, both before specific training is begun and while it is being carried on. They are used in connection with each language form which the child is trained to lipread and use. Specific training in lipreading sentences is also valuable in showing the child that a toy, an activity, or a picture may be described in a number of ways.

The first specific sentence work probably begins about the time the child is learning to match pictures illustrating activities which may be described in such sentences as, "The boy is running," "The man is driving a car," "The woman is carrying a baby," "The girl is playing with a dog," and others. He also learns to match, and eventually to lipread, simple sentences using *has* and *have;* for example, "The boy has a ball," "The woman has a baby," "The girl has a dog," and so on.

As the child progresses from the three-year-old level to the four, and then to the five, the sentences increase in number and in length, and become increasingly challenging, as his vocabulary expands and his experiences are spoken of in different ways.

Many colorful pictures and charts are needed for practice in sentence work. The adult finds it necessary to assemble a collection of useful, interesting pictures. Each picture may be mounted, or clipped to medium-weight paper of a neutral shade. The pictures should be catalogued in folders, or systematically numbered, so both child and adult are able to find a wanted picture quickly. There will be pictures that provide for practice in the use of each verb, each preposition, and other language forms in sentences. Pictures may be collected and catalogued according to whether they illustrate holiday activities, home activities of child and family, school activities, activities of community workers (the postman, the garageman, the storekeeper, the milkman, the policeman, etc.), special excursions and trips (to the zoo, to the beach, to the mountains, to the library, etc.), places of interest in the community (the post office, the docks, the fire-station, the city hall, the farm, the department store, the drugstore, etc.), and others.

As the child becomes more familiar with lipreading, the adult purposely changes the wording of a sentence so the child will be able to get the thought of the sentence whether it is constructed in one way or another.

The sentence work is planned and presented as a progression from the simple to the more difficult, and the adult must be constantly aware of the fact that the child is still very young. To present such a group of sentences as, "The boy is eating peas," "The boy is eating beans," "The boy is eating beets," in one lesson would be quite unreasonable. *Peas, beans,* and *beets,* look exactly alike on the lips, and even the most expert adult lipreader would have difficulty in understanding which of the three words was being used.

The five-year-old who has had two or three years of previous training often understands that certain words look alike on the lips; and there are some children who enjoy being given words which look alike, and who have fun in trying to guess which word is being said. However, since most children of this age are not so sophisticated about language, it is up to the adult to make each lesson in sentences interesting and challenging without being either frustrating or discouraging. It is possible for two sentences which sound different, and whose meanings are different, to look fairly similar on the lips. The child should learn to lipread such sentences, but should not be required to work in the most difficult manner.

Some deaf children at the preschool level have learned to lipread sentences by watching the side of the speaker's face. Four-year-olds have begun to do this. They have been exposed to the sentences as the adult allows them to watch the full face, the face at an angle of about forty-five degrees, and then the side of the face.

Certainly, this elaboration of the usual lipreading is not a *must.* No child should have to strain to interpret spoken language in this way. However, if the matter is well-managed in an offhand way, the little deaf child can enjoy these variations. If he does, even though he is not expected to become expert at "lipreading from the side," the exercise helps to make him more aware of muscles, and of movements of other parts of the face besides the lips.

The child should have practice in lipreading sentences from other angles; for example, when the face of the speaker is above his eye level, and below his eye level. Such practice, of course, should take place only when the child has become familiar with lipreading when the adult's face is on a level with his.

Whenever sentences are used, the child should be encouraged to say them with the adult, or to imitate them. As he progresses in lipreading and imitation of speech, he should be encouraged to use sentences spontaneously in describing familiar pictures.

In the child's use of the sentence, the rhythm of the *whole sentence* is more important than the pronunciation of individual words in the sentence. As he gets more practice and encouragement in saying sentences rhythmically, his speech becomes even more intelligible.

148

As his speech improves and he becomes familiar with the speech pattern of the sentences, more attention may be given to certain words in the sentence. This part of the training of the young deaf child should be in the hands of an expert. A wrong move here may destroy much of the earlier, hard-earned progress. The skilled teacher will know how to strike a balance among articulation, fluency of speech, and the maintaining of a good voice quality (in so far as this is possible for a deaf child), these three elements in the right proportion being essential in developing intelligible speech. The skilled teacher never sacrifices fluency, meanings, or voice quality for articulation, for example—a regrettable misplacing of emphasis which could take place when the child is at the preschool levels.

Parents should be aware of such dangers, especially those who are determined to "do something" about speech development in their respective children. Some parents resent being told to restrict their speech work with their respective children to the imitation of speech, and often resent the fact that the teachers aren't "doing more about" *speech*. There are good reasons for the teacher's way of approaching speech. In spite of much authentic, well-founded advice, there have been parents who have unwisely taken things into their own hands, and then, when their children started to school, the teachers had to begin "at the bottom" to try to repair the damages done, and the parents were utterly bewildered by a situation which they themselves created.[159]

These matters are discussed here since the use of sentences— or misuse of them—by the children frequently disturbs the parents; and as they are struck by the realization that to give language and speech to the deaf child seems an almost hopeless, and certainly a tremendous, undertaking, their anxiety may drive them on to what they call "action."

When a child uses a succession of nouns, or one or two nouns and a verb, in attempting to make a sentence, to tell the parent something, to ask for something, the child should not be discouraged nor made to feel that no one is satisfied to try to understand him as he is and as he talks. He should not be subjected to extreme corrective measures, nor be forced to "say that word better." If the situation lends itself to casual correction, as many do, the parent may repeat what the child has tried to say, using the appropriate language. Then, if the child will repeat the sentence, he should be given approval and a response. The same principle applies in the more specific work which the parent may carry on in lipreading and use of sentences.

The value of the child's willingness to lipread and say a sentence *as a whole* must not be vitiated by stopping him in his effort, by manipulating his lips and tongue, by drilling on a particular word or consonant. This kind of meddling, aside from the harmful psychological effects, results in the stilted, "one-word-at-a-time," jerky speech, which so many parents react to in listening to some deaf children talking.

A great deal of sentence work may be done in conjunction with auditory training, and this is discussed at some length under Auditory Training Activities for Language Development (page 176).

QUESTIONS AND ANSWERS

The ability to understand questions by lipreading, to answer, and to ask questions is a goal which parents and teachers hope the deaf child will reach as early as possible. The deaf child who has learned to ask and answer questions has come a long way. When he is able to use language in this manner, he is using speech as a social activity; and he is rapidly nearing the stage where he may use speech in "influencing the behavior of those about him," [82] a use to which speech is put by the majority in society.

Questions and answers cause confusion and frustration for many deaf children, especially when the need to use these language forms confronts them in social situations in and out of the home, and in lessons on almost every academic subject. A foundation should be laid in the preschool years which can help to obviate such problems. Preschool training in question and answer work will not eliminate all possibility of future language problems caused by questions and answers, but it should help child and adult in meeting those problems and resolving them more readily.

Parent and teacher begin asking the child questions from the time his training is begun. Needless to say, the adult has to do both the asking and the answering for some time. Simple questions such as, "Who is that?" or "Where is Mother?" arise many times during a child's day, and although the child cannot answer since he doesn't understand the significance of the question, the person who has asked the question should help the child to bridge the gap between question and answer by answering aloud as the child watches. In time, the child begins to see a relationship between the question and the answer.

The four-year-old who has had a year or two of previous training may begin to answer some simple questions. In the beginning, he may indicate an understanding of the question by some action rather than by speech, if he hasn't grasped the idea of responding with spontaneous speech. The adult will accept his means of response and at the same time will assist him to use the appropriate words.

After the child has had considerable experience in lipreading and in imitating speech, he may begin to repeat the question which the adult asks; and, when she gives him the answer, he will repeat it, too.[119] If the child follows the "normal" channels of language development, he will go through this stage. Occasionally, the adult is more confused by this development than the child is. The adult who "fusses" about it and tries to clarify the situation by "logical" explanations, or by stopping the child in his imitating, will find the situation becoming more and more confusing for her and the child.

As the child is going through this stage of imitating both question and answer, he is taking note of other factors. He begins to notice that every time the speaker says, "What color," the word, "red," "blue," or some other color is used; that every time the speaker says, "*Who* is that?" a person is referred to; and so on. He must be given time to recognize these relationships through much daily practice in general and specific situations.

Later on, the adult will find that, as soon as the child imitates the question she has asked, he quickly gives the answer without any assistance. At this point, question games are introduced, in which the child asks the questions and the adult gives the answers. Before long, the child realizes that one person asks the question and the other person responds.

It takes a long time for the child to acquire the knowledge and the language that enable him to answer and ask questions of the simplest variety, in spite of the many situations that lend themselves to such practice.

Number work furnishes practice in lipreading and using the question form *How many;* color work offers opportunity to practice the question form *What color;* work with nouns provides for the use of *What's that,* or *Who is that;* preposition work for *Where;* activities bring forth questions such as *What happened, Did you go down town, What did you do,* etc.

Question games provide an enjoyable way of learning to lipread various question forms and to answer them. A child might hide a few objects about the room while the adult covers her eyes. Then the adult will ask, "*Where* did you hide the ball?" or "*Where* is the airplane?" or "*Where* did you put the gun?" and the child would answer, using the appropriate phrase.

In a group of children, each one might be given a toy which he hides behind his back. The adult may ask, "Who has the ball?" The child who has the ball would bring it into view and say, "I have." Or, one child might be asked to guess who has the ball, who has the book, who has the drum, etc., and would respond with the name of the child who has the particular object.

The child who has had adequate language experiences should be given every opportunity to ask questions, and this often means that the child becomes the teacher, and the teacher the pupil who must answer. This technique is usually very successful with five-year-olds.

THE TIME ELEMENT

The parent often finds herself faced with the problem of explaining to the child that something will happen tomorrow, or at some other time. The little deaf child often wonders why one child has the pretty birthday cake with candles placed before him, and when his turn will come. He may wonder why windows in the stores display a big man in a red suit and what all this will mean for him. He may have some understanding of Christmas in terms of Santa Claus and gifts, and as soon as he sees Christmas decorations and pictures he may want his Santa Claus gifts immediately.

Daily use of the calendar at home and at school (if the child is in nursery school) helps to put across the idea of time, and the child begins to understand that, even though he may not like it and regardless of anything he may do, he must wait until the special day arrives.

Large calendars should be used with ample white space around the numbers, so that, next to each printed date, a small drawing of a birthday cake, a Christmas tree, an Easter rabbit, may be inserted, to denote the *time* for special occasions.[35]

Each month usually offers a holiday or some festive occasion, and the child begins to notice that, as each day is crossed off, the special day draws nearer. The adult uses terms such as *today, tomorrow, yesterday, in three days*, etc., and uses the calendar to explain what she means.

The preschool deaf child has very little understanding of the terms *today, tomorrow,* and *yesterday*. The preschool hearing child constantly confuses them. Nevertheless, the adult uses the terms without expecting the child to use them. The deaf child does begin to understand the difference between *a long time* and *in a little while*. Many a parent has discovered that the young deaf child—like the hearing child—becomes quite "skilled" in the use of such phrases as *after a while* or *in a minute* as means of putting off something which he has been asked to do. One five-year-old child who had been begging her mother and father to take her to the beach and who had been told many times, "After a while," instead of being given a definite answer, one day responded with, "After a while. All the time, after a while." The child soon learns that time terms may be used by both adults *and children* in delaying actions and activities.

Calendars may also be used for language work in connection with the weather from day to day. Four- and five-year-olds usually enjoy this. If the day is sunny, the adult, and later on, the child, might draw a picture of the sun beside the date; and the sentence, "The sun is shining," would be practiced for lipreading and speech. If it is raining, a picture of rain and an umbrella might be drawn beside the number; and the sentence, "It is raining," would be practiced. Other weather language, such as *It is cloudy, It is hot, It is cold,* may be practiced in a similar manner.

The child's day follows a certain pattern—time for school, time for lunch, time to go home, time to go to bed, etc.—and the child enjoys learning to identify these times with certain positions of the hands of the clock. The adult might make a large cardboard clock with movable hands. The hands might be set at lunch time, twelve o'clock, and when the hands of the real clock on the wall reach the same position, the child is shown that they are the same and that it is time for lunch.

If the child, impatient about going downtown, must wait another five minutes, the adult would tell him, "We'll leave in five minutes," and show him five minutes on the clock. In most cases, the child keeps an eye on the clock, and in five minutes is back to remind the adult that it's time to leave.

With the best of training, the preschool deaf child's understanding of time is limited, but he can acquire some understanding which makes life much more comfortable for him and his parents, and which makes future language work with time simpler and more interesting for him.

STORIES, AND PICTURE DESCRIPTIONS

Specific work with stories and picture descriptions, which demands a background of general experience with language and storytelling, seldom begins before the child's last year in preschool when he is five or six years old. Up to this time, the child should have had many experiences with the common stories of childhood, and with pictures that have been described to him over and over again in various ways. (Plate XIII)

When the child is ready, specific steps may be taken through the use of familiar stories to impress upon the child that there is a *sequence* of events in each story. For example, the child doesn't understand the story of *Jack and Jill* if he thinks that Jack fell down the hill before he went up. Probably the child has had some experience in pantomiming the story and has established some notion of the sequence. In order to ensure a correct idea of sequence, the adult would have a series of pictures, each picture illustrating a specific step. The pictures would be presented to the child one at a time, described in a simple sentence, and placed side by side on a ledge or in a slot chart until the whole story is told in pictures.

After all the pictures are in place, with the first picture on the left, the last on the right, each one is described. The child is encouraged to describe each picture, using the sentence which the adult has used. Then the pictures might be removed, mixed up, and handed to the child, who proceeds to put them back in the chart or on the ledge in the correct order. As he becomes more and more adept at doing this, he might be asked to talk about each picture as he places it.[36]

The adult might collect a series of pictures that illustrate a trip to the store. One picture would be of the child being given money by his mother; the next picture might be of him walking towards the store; the next, of him walking into the store; the next, of him buying an article from the storekeeper and paying for it; the next, of him walking home; the last, of him giving it to his mother. Pictures of this sort may be drawn or may be found in the prereading books available in bookstores.

It must be made clear that stories should not be analyzed on the level of much older children. The training should be fun and can be fun. The story is told using colorful, attractive pictures; it is pantomimed and dramatized, and the individual pictures would be described and placed in proper sequence. After this has been done, questions on the story may be asked.

This work is extremely important. The child's understanding of the sequence of events, of the fact that one thing must happen before another event occurs, has a definite bearing on the quality of work he will do in the grades. He will be better equipped to get the thought of a whole story or paragraph, spoken or read, and to answer questions regarding it with greater ease.

Stories may be developed from the children's excursions, using blackboard drawings and sketches or pictures from magazines and children's books. The child should be encouraged to say anything he wants to say about the excursion or the picture. When all the interesting incidents of the excursion have been discussed informally, the adult reorganizes them into story form, and, using the illustration, talks to the child and encourages him in his attempts to tell a story.

The success attained through these story-games, which are designed to promote logical thought along with language skills, will depend on the skill with which the teacher or the parent guides the child. The child must be happy in the situation, and in addition, there must be guidance and an aim.

Photo by Ross Madden   *Courtesy John Tracy Clinic*

PLATE XIII.—Child watches the lips as his mother tells him a story using pictures in the book.

CHAPTER 12

Auditory Training Activities
for Language Development

In the use of the activities described in this section, the adult will find it necessary to "try out" various exercises casually, especially for the very young deaf child. This training should be as regular as possible, but, in the early stages, it is not very systematic. It must become systematic, but first of all, the child needs time to feel comfortable with the new techniques, to adjust to the various demands which auditory training makes on him, and to "find his way" into this unusual experience through the exercises which appear to be most pleasant for him.[95]

Some young children like to move from one activity to another; others prefer one in particular, and want to do it over and over again. The adult often finds herself in the position of having to meet the child's preferences and at the same time channel the preferences to make the training effective.

As the child adjusts to the whole situation and begins to enjoy the sound, however he may "hear" it, and its implications for him, the training can become more systematic. The child's individuality in this matter plays a powerful role in determining the degree to which the child will accept the adult's direction and to which auditory training may help him.[31]

TALKING AND SINGING

Among the first things that the parent and the teacher may do in training the young deaf child are to sing and talk near his ear.[223] This is done, to the child's advantage, from the time his deafness is discovered and before he is ready for earphones or a wearable aid. And much later on, after specific training has been started, every opportunity should be grasped to utter near his ear a word, a phrase, a tune, etc. This technique, which is as simple as it is effective, may be carried out while the child is lying down, while he is looking at books and pictures, during the speech and lipreading lessons, and on many other incidental occasions during the day. If the child doesn't respond, the adult does not make an issue of it, nor try to make him respond.

This method is very helpful in encouraging some children to "use voice." A child may try to imitate a word which he sees on the lips of a speaker, but in doing so may not use his voice. Sometimes, if the child's hand is placed on the speaker's cheek as the word is said near his ear, and then again while he watches, he will repeat the word using voice.

Talking and singing are usually natural and pleasant experiences for any child, and for the deaf child can be just as pleasant.[136]

Earphones may be attached to the radio, or if the child is learning to use a wearable aid, he might put it on, and he would have an opportunity to listen to music and to people talking. The child may prefer listening to music rather than to talking, and this preference should be recognized and encouraged.

If he is listening to music, the adult should have pictures of the various instruments on hand, and when a particular instrument is being played, the corresponding picture would be displayed.

One parent constructed a scrapbook of musical instruments and kept it in the record cabinet. When the child "listened" to the music, with earphones, with a wearable aid, or just by touching the radio with his hands and placing his ear against the side of the cabinet, he and his mother would look through the scrapbook for the picture of the particular instrument he was "hearing."

If the child will listen to people talking over the radio, he should have an opportunity to become familiar with the speech of a man, of a woman, or of a child, and pictures of these people should be available for such occasions.

GROSS SOUNDS

Using gross sounds provides another way of testing the child's hearing and of helping to make him conscious of different sounds such as those produced by a bass drum, a toy drum, a toy whistle, a police whistle, a dinner bell, a cow bell, a bicycle bell, a toy cricket, a cymbal, a motor horn, and various pitch pipes.[57] (Plate XIV)

The adult should be cautioned against over-using this exercise. In many cases, the adult, finding that the child responds to a certain sound, from then on plagues the child with the sound until he gives up any hope of relief from it and decides that he doesn't want to hear it or anything else.

While it is quite important that the child be exposed to as much sound as possible, since the use of sounds may promote speech and lipreading responses, it is also important that the adult realize how annoying to a young deaf child the constant ringing of bells and banging of drums can become, especially since the persistent ringer of the bell usually insists upon some response over and over again. Such persistence can result in auditory training losing all its value. A child may even get into the habit of saying that he "hears" everything in the auditory training and testing situation, because he has come to believe that is all the adult wants of him.

When the child is able to respond to two or three of the gross sounds, the adult begins to use those responses systematically in training the child to indicate which of the two sounds he heard. For example, after the child has listened to a drum and

PLATE XIV.—Child learning to respond to gross sounds. Mother assists.

a pitch pipe, in game and other play situations, frequently enough to be able to respond and to know that those sounds came from those toys, both toys might be placed before the child. The adult would strike the drum while the child watches and listens; then blow the pitch pipe while the child watches and listens. Then the child is turned around; one of the sounds would be produced; and the child would turn back to the adult and indicate which of the toys was the source of the sound. The child may need assistance for some time in learning what to do, and in learning to differentiate between two sounds. (Plate XIV)

The next exercise might consist of learning to discriminate, by hearing, between the drum and the cymbal; the next, between the pitch pipe and the cymbal; and so on until he has had a great deal of experience in differentiating between two sounds.

The next step would include work with three gross sounds, in which the child is trained to indicate which of the three toys in front of him was the source of the sound he "heard."

In accordance with the child's readiness and his capacity to "hear" the sounds, more and more gross sounds would be used in each lesson. There are three-year-olds who have learned to discriminate among a number of gross sounds, while some children will need all the preschool years to learn to discriminate between two or three.

The names of the toys used may be given to the child, and although the training with the sound of a drum need not imply that the child will say the word "drum" more intelligibly, there is a possibility that it will help in this respect, and certainly the child's understanding the word is broadened through this experience that has taken place in connection with it. (Plate XV)

These exercises may be carried out with and without amplification. If amplification is employed, it should not be so great that the sound would reach the child in blasts, even for a child who is suspected of being severely deaf and who, at the time, appears

Photo by Ross Madden   *Courtesy John Tracy Clinic*

PLATE XV.—Deaf child responding to gross sound (drum) by knocking down blocks.

to have very little if any residual hearing. The amplification should be increased gradually to avoid discomfort and shock.

VOWEL SOUNDS

From the time the child was first exposed to spoken language, he was also, in a general way, exposed to vowel sounds as they occur in words. Vowel sounds are usually the first sounds uttered by the child when he begins to imitate speech. In order to encourage the use of these vowels, in words, babbling, and speech play, to make the child acquainted with "how they sound," and because some of them are relatively easy to imitate and to see on the lips, vowels are incorporated into the auditory training exercises. This work appears to be more effective for the young child when the vowels are presented in animal sounds, such as *bow-wow, moo, baa,* etc. (Plate XVI)

The child must be given considerable practice in listening to these sounds as related to the toy animals and to the pictures of the animals as they are used in sense training, lipreading, and speech activities. Later, when he shows some understanding of the relationship between the animal and the sound, he may begin to differentiate between two of the sounds.

The adult might place a toy dog and a toy cow on a table before the child. A mirror might be hung behind the table, directly before the child. The adult would point to the dog and would say, as the child listens, places his hand on her face, and watches in the mirror, "The dog says, 'Bow-wow,' 'Bow-wow,' 'Bow-wow.' " As the child imitates *bow-wow,* he and the adult would clap, once for *Bow* and once for *wow,* in the same rhythm as the spoken word. The same procedure would be followed for a cow and the sound *moo.*

Then the child would be turned away from the mirror and the adult; and as he listens, the adult says one of the sounds near his ear, or into the microphone. The child turns back to the table

164

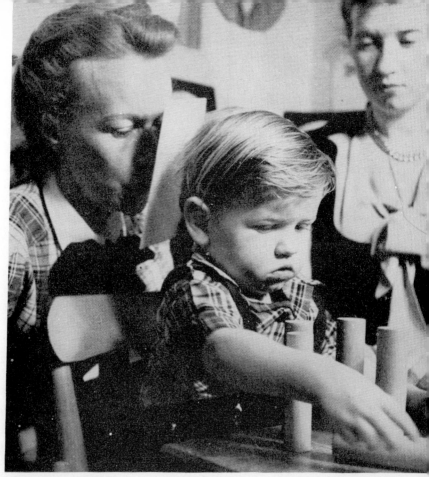

Photo by Ross Madden   *Courtesy John Tracy Clinic*

PLATE XVI.—A two-year-old learning to respond to vowel sounds.

and indicates which sound he "heard," by pointing to the animal and repeating the sound. (Plate XVII)

It must be understood that, although these exercises may provide a lot of fun for the deaf child, reliable responses may be very slow in developing. The child is given support in these exercises by the adult's acceptance of his attempts and responses, and by using two sounds that differ in number of syllables; for example, *Bow-wow,* two syllables, *Moo,* one.

There are instances where a child, after months or even a year or two of daily training, does not differentiate between two such sounds with any reliability. But the same child, through the constant practice he has had, has learned to say the sounds intelligibly, and has learned to say sentences such as, "The dog says, 'Bow-wow,' " with some intelligibility and much understanding, and is able to answer questions such as, "What says, 'Bow-wow'?"

The child sometimes enjoys looking through magazines to find and cut out, with the adult's help, advertisements illustrating people using such sounds as $\bar{oo}, \bar{o},$ etc., and the pictures may be used with such remarks as, "The woman is saying, '$\bar{O}\bar{o}$, the coffee is good!' " "I can say $\bar{oo}$ just the way the woman says it. Let me hear you say $\bar{oo}$." The child might watch himself in the mirror as he tries to match his lip formations with those of the woman in the picture.[135]

Drills on single vowels are not recommended. They are meaningless to the child, and there are so many interesting ways of using vowels that such drills are not necessary.

PIANO

When the parent and the teacher have access to a piano or organ, they should use it in the training of the young deaf child.[75] Some of the deafest children, after daily experience in watching, feeling, and "listening" with earphones, have learned to recognize differences between high and low chords, fast music and slow, loud and soft. They enjoy listening and feeling music

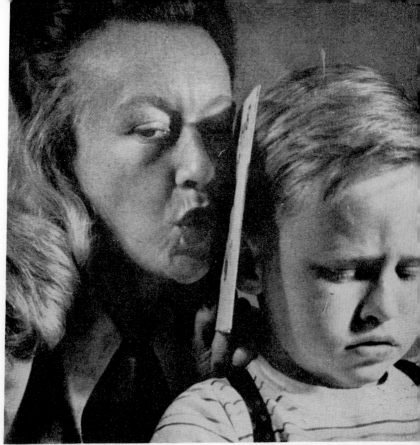

Photo by Ross Madden   *Courtesy John Tracy Clinic*

PLATE XVII.—Child listening and feeling animal sound before
indicating corresponding animal.

Courtesy John Tracy Clinic

PLATE XVIII.—Deaf child listens (earphones), feels piano and watches as teacher plays "high" and "low" chords on piano. Child

turns away, listens and feels as chords are replayed. Indicates whether "high" or "low" chord was played by raising (left) or lowering (right) hand and saying the word "high" or "low."

that represents running, falling, jumping, and other actions, and have learned to recognize the music that goes with a particular action.

The young deaf child should have regular practice in counting chords played, clapping in time to the music. As three chords are played, he claps his hands three times, once for each chord. As he progresses, he learns to say the numbers as he claps. Since counting and clapping involve considerable preparation, the child should not be expected to master these activities in a short time. It would be an error to sacrifice the rhythm in the child's attempts at keeping time to the music, whether he uses his voice or claps his hands, either for the sake of articulation in saying the numbers or for the sake of clapping his hands in perfect time.

Some children enjoy knocking over blocks to music. If one chord is played, he knocks over one block; two chords, two blocks; and so on. He needs direction and a great deal of time to accomplish this exercise, which may appear relatively simple to the adult.

The deaf child has enjoyed babbling to piano music, matching his babbling to the tempo of the music, or babbling softly to soft music and loud to loud music. Piano work, along with the tactile and auditory techniques, has been effective in training deaf children to vary the pitch of their voices in using words, and has helped the child to use words with more normal inflection. (Plate XVIII)

Speech work involving whole words, phrases, and sentences may be effectively pursued in conjunction with the piano and the hearing aid. From the adult's using spoken language as she plays the piano, the child gets an excellent experience of "listening" to the rhythm of speech in conjunction with the rhythm of music.

The degree of response will depend a great deal on the age, the hearing deficiency, the maturity, the personality, and the previous training of each child. The adult should be much more concerned with what daily exposure to these exercises, as a whole, do for the child than with the precision or promptness, or specific nature of his responses to them. The very fact that the child is deaf will limit him in his responses to piano work, especially as to clapping, counting, talking, etc., *in time* to the piano music. At the preschool level, the sensory experiences he gains from the piano work are extremely valuable. A rigid, technical approach to it could be harmful.

PHONOGRAPH

The phonograph is used by teachers and parents to give the child practice in listening to different kinds of music, to train him to know when the music is "on" or "off," and to train him to recognize one instrument from another in so far as this is possible. (Plate XIX)

Whenever possible, the child should have the opportunity of seeing the real instruments he hears through the phonograph, and of feeling them as they are being played. Then, while listening to the recording, the real or the pictured instrument or both would be displayed.[118]

After the child has had much practice and experience in listening to two of the instruments, he may be able to indicate which of the two is being played.

Some deaf children have learned to identify four or five instruments; others only one or two, even after a few years of training. But almost every child can learn that the music is "on" or "off"; can be made aware of sound in another way, and therefore more conscious of his environment as a whole.

WORDS

In training the child to differentiate between and interpret words through listening, the same words would be used as have been used from the beginning in the combined speech, lipread-

PLATE XIX.—1. Child learns when phonograph is "on" and "off," by listening, feeling and watching.

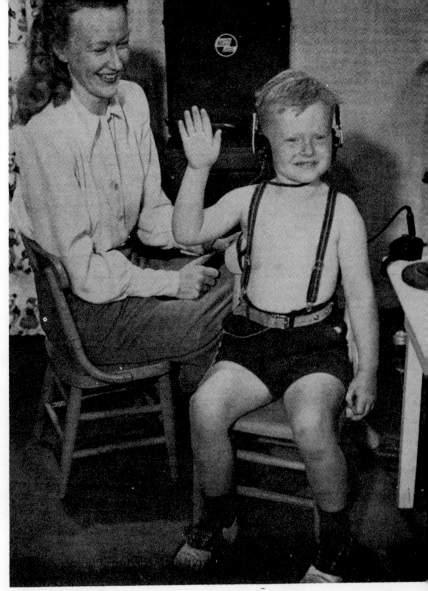

Photo by Ross Madden　　　　　　　　　　*Courtesy John Tracy Clinic*

PLATE XIX.—2. Child indicates by raising hand that he "hears" the music.

ing, and auditory training lessons. The more familiar a child is with a word, the faster he will learn to understand it in new situations.

The first two words chosen might be those which differ as to number of syllables in each; for example, *shoe* and *airplane*.

The chosen words would be repeated several times, as the child watches and listens and imitates. He would be guided in clapping to each word—once for the one-syllable word, twice for the two-syllable word—and where one syllable in a word is accented, he would clap loudly, the unaccented syllable being accompanied by a light clap. The more differences he is able to recognize in the two words, the better.

The next step would be to let the child listen without the help of lipreading or the tactile expression. Immediately after saying the word under these conditions, the adult permits the child to see her face as she repeats the word. The second word would be treated in a like manner. Then, covering her whole face, or just her mouth, the adult would say one of the words into the microphone, and the child would try to tell her, by indicating the corresponding picture and repeating the word himself, what was said.

This exercise requires concentration on the part of the child, and patience and ingenuity on the part of the adult, in order to keep the child interested. The exercise is valuable, regardless of how inexpert the child may remain at differentiating between words by auditory means alone. He is being exposed to spoken language every time the lesson occurs; he gets more practice with the particular language forms used, in listening to others speak. and in listening to his own voice.

Several different pairs of words may be introduced as the child begins to understand what is expected of him and as his skill increases in differentiating between the words of the one pair used in the first lessons. Some deaf children never get beyond differentiating between two words at one time. Others learn to

Photo by Ross Madden   Courtesy John Tracy Clinic

PLATE XX.—Severely deaf child listens as teacher says a word to correspond with a picture on table. Parents observe and record.

identify any one of several words through listening alone. (Plates XX, XXI)

SENTENCES

The child is exposed to simple sentences from the beginning days of his training. As soon as he will wear earphones, he listens to these sentences as he lipreads, tries to imitate them and to match them to corresponding pictures. After he has had a great deal of experience in lipreading, in imitating, and in listening to sentences, two which he understands very well, and which differ as to length and number of accented and unaccented syllables, would be used in training him to differentiate between sentences through listening alone.[213]

This type of exercise requires concentration and undivided attention on the part of the child. He will continue to try only if he feels that the adult is helping him and is not forcing him to "do it or else." (Plate XXII)

In differentiating between sentences, the procedure is similar to that in differentiating between words. If the sentences (with corresponding pictures) are, *The woman has some flowers,* and *The boy is crying,* each sentence would be repeated several times by the adult, while the child watches, lipreads, indicates the corresponding picture, and then imitates. The child may be made more aware of the differences in the sentences if he watches the adult clap as she says each sentence, and claps along with her. The sentences should be spoken' with normal fluency, not in artificial, choppy style: one word—a pause—another word.

Then the adult would cover her face, or just her mouth in the first stages, as she says one of the sentences into the microphone; and the child would try to indicate the correct picture and to repeat the sentence.

A short time devoted each day to this exercise, in conjunction with speech and lipreading, is more valuable to the preschool

Photo by Ross Madden　　　　　　　　*Courtesy John Tracy Clinic*

PLATE XXI.–Child indicates picture which corresponds with the words he "hears."

child than long lessons that are only empty drills, which the child forgets as fast as he can.

After the child has learned to differentiate between the sentences in several pairs, he may be able to differentiate among three familiar sentences. There are deaf children who have learned to indicate which one of several pictures was described, just through listening. And although such children were far too deaf to use hearing as a means of understanding people in their environments, there was a definite improvement in their speech and lipreading. There was also an outstanding improvement in the articulation of those sentences which were used for auditory training. The more sentences that can be used in such exercises, and the more practice the child gets in saying them, the more greatly his articulation will improve—as well as his accent and fluency—without articulation having to be specifically worked on in those lessons.

This work with sentences at the preschool level has value that lasts far into the later years. However, for highest effectiveness, it should be continued well past the preschool level.

NURSERY RHYMES AND JINGLES

Deaf children should be exposed to the rhymes and jingles which hearing children enjoy. Hearing children have at first relatively little understanding of the rhymes and stories they hear, but they enjoy them anyway and want to hear them over and over again. If they are made interesting, the deaf child feels the same about them.

The adult tries to put across the *idea* of the rhyme while she gives the child some experience with the rhythm of the language of the rhyme. In time, the child learns the names of the people and things in the rhymes, and to "talk" with the adult into the microphone as the whole rhyme is repeated.

The deaf child enjoys recordings of the nursery rhymes, likes to have pictures of them to go with the recordings, and will clap

PLATE XXII.—Severely deaf child listens, watches side of speaker's face in mirror as pictures on table are described in sentences, and indicates corresponding pictures.

and try to sing with the adult as the recording is being played.

Deaf children at the preschool level have learned to differentiate between nursery rhymes, spoken or played on the victrola, through listening alone. There are others who have to lipread at the same time they listen in order to interpret or differentiate, and where this is the case, they should not be deprived of the chance to lipread. Auditory training, although it has been designed to train the hearing handicapped to make fullest use of whatever hearing they possess, cannot change the deaf child into a hearing child. The adult who uses auditory training only to "make" deaf children hear, or who uses it only with those children whom she believes able to hear "something," is not the person to be training young deaf children.[155]

Auditory training can be discouragingly slow. In the case of young deaf children, it may go on for months and months before auditory responses of a reliable nature are noticed. Sometimes, there is apparently no response. Nevertheless, auditory training plays an important role in the development of speech and lipreading. Even when it may not improve language skills, it can contribute indirectly to language skills by making the language which the child must learn to *use* a much more meaningful tool.[100]

CHAPTER 13

Suggested Outlines for Language Lessons

The following outlines are presented for the purpose of giving the adult in charge additional guidance in the use of activities suggested in previous chapters. There is always some danger in presenting such outlines since they have been known to be misused. However, these suggestions should be helpful in concretizing for the adult the steps involved in various lessons for language development. All value is lost unless the guidance of the child is based on his own patterns of thinking and feeling. Any suggested procedure must be subject to change and used in accordance with the manifestations of the individual child.

SUGGESTION 1

Aim

To familiarize the child with consonants *p, b,* and *m,* in words beginning with these consonants, and in words presented as concepts. The tactile, visual, and auditory means would be employed for the promotion of lipreading, speech, and auditory responses.

Materials

Individual, colorful pictures of familiar words—a pie, a pig, a boy, a ball, milk, a man.

Pictures of activities revolving about the above nouns; for

example, a picture of a boy with a ball, a picture of a man with a pig, etc.

A mirror and a hearing aid.

Procedure

(1) Child and adult seated before a table of comfortable height for child, with mirror behind table and directly in front of adult and child.

(2) Pictures of a pie and a pig placed on table.

(3) Child's hand is placed on adult's cheek. Child watches in mirror while adult, holding up the picture of the pie, says, "That's a *pie*. A pie."

(4) Adult repeats sentence and word near the child's ear, while he watches in mirror.

(5) One of child's hands is placed on adult's cheek, the other on his own cheek, and he is encouraged to say the sentence and the word with the adult, as both watch the procedure in the mirror.

(6) The same procedure is followed using the word *pig*.

(7) Adult asks the child, "Where is the pig?" "Show me the pie." Child lipreads and indicates the appropriate picture. He is encouraged to say the word when he indicates the picture.

(8) Same procedure followed, using words *boy* and *ball;* then *milk* and *man.*

(9) Place on the table a picture of a *pie*, one of a *boy*, and one of a *man*. (*p, b,* and *m* all look alike on the lips, but do not sound alike.)

(10) Adult uses the three words, as the child watches, feels, and listens.

(11) Introduce activity pictures or those which illustrate the particular objects in relation to other objects or people. Place earphones on child and set volume control. Describe each picture simply as child watches, listens, and feels (visual, tactile, auditory); for example, "The *boy* has a *ball*." "The *boy* has a

pie." "The boy has a pig." "The boy has some milk." "The man has a pie." "The man has a ball." "The man has some milk." "The man has a pig." Pictures may be described in other ways; such as, "The boy is playing with a ball," etc.

(12) Some or all of pictures may be described again while adult and child clap to the rhythm of the sentence, accenting key words; for example, "The boy has a ball." Child is encouraged to speak as he claps. Movements and use of voice should be rhythmical.

Note.—The above exercise is meant to be general. More specific work with the consonants *p, b,* and *m* develops out of such a general approach. The very specific work with such sounds should be in the hands of a *trained* person.

SUGGESTION 2

Aim

To familiarize the child with consonants *t* and *d* in words and sentences and in babbling exercises. The tactile, visual, and auditory means would be combined wherever possible.

Materials

Objects such as a top, a toy table, a doll, and a toy dog. A hearing aid.

Procedure

(1) Child places one hand on adult's cheek, one on his own cheek. Adult says the following babbling sounds and child repeats: dŭdŭdŭ, dŏdŏdŏ, dōōdōōdōō, dēēdeedee, tŏtŏtŏ, tēētēētēē, tātātā, tătătă.

(2) Adult and child babble and say a word related to the babbling exercise; for example: dŏdŏdŏ—dŏg; dŏdŏdŏ—dŏll; tŏtŏtŏ—tŏp; tātātā—tāble, etc.

(3) Incorporate some activity by having the child carry out instructions through lipreading; for example: "Put the top on the table," "Put the doll on the table," etc.

(4) Place the four pictures on the table before the child. Adult points to each and asks, "What's that?" Child is guided in saying, "A top," "A table," "A dog," etc.

(5) In the case of the child who has some language understanding, the adult might use the following: "What's that?" Child answers, with or without help, "A table." "Is that a dog?" (pointing to the top), and child answers "No, a top," etc.

SUGGESTION 3

Aim

To familiarize the child with the consonant *f* in whole words, phrases, and sentences using tactile, visual, and auditory means.

Materials

Objects (a fish, a flower).
Pictures (a fish, a flower).
A paper bag, a slot chart, and a box large enough to hold objects.
A hearing aid.

Procedure

(1) Adult shows the toy fish to the child, places child's hand on her cheek, and says, "Here is a *f*ish. A *f*ish." Child places other hand on his own cheek and says the word. (Same procedure for *flower*.)

(2) Both objects are placed on the table. Adult says, "Show me the *fish*." Child indicates correct object, and says "Fish," with or without help from the adult. (Same procedure for *flower*.)

(3) Lipreading—"Put the *fish* in the bag." "Put the *flower* in the bag." The bag may be held towards the child to help him in understanding what is meant, until he has had more practice with the activity and the language.

(4) Child is asked to find each of the objects by reaching into the bag without looking (touch only). "Find the *fish*." Child feels the objects in the bag and pulls out the fish. After the adult

184

asks, "What's that?" the child says, "A *fish*." (Same procedure for *flower*.)

(5) Remove the paper bag and place the box on the table. Adult "hides" one of the objects with her hands, and says, "Guess what I have in my hands," or "What do I have, a fish or a flower?" Child "guesses"; and when he "guesses" correctly and says the word, the adult says, "Put the *fish* in the box," and "Put the *flower* in the box." The child may be allowed to "hide" the objects, for the adult to "guess."

(6) Pictures of the flower and the fish would be introduced and the child would lipread, "Show me the picture of the *flower*." He indicates the correct picture and says, "*Flower*," or "That's a *flower*." (Similar procedure for *fish*.)

(7) Pictures and objects would be placed on table, and the child would lipread, "Show me a *flower*." "Show me another flower." "Show me a fish." "Show me another fish." . . . "Yes, that's a *flower*, and that's a *flower*. That's a *fish* and that's a fish." (Adult might point to the flower and say, "Is that a *fish*?" Child would be guided in saying, "No, a *flower*.")

(8) Pictures of a fish and a flower are placed in a slot chart hanging near child. The child might play "teacher." The adult would turn her back to the child and he would say one of the words, or, if he has had more training, might be able to use a simple sentence such as "Show me the fish." If the speech is relatively intelligible, the adult turns and points to the picture of the fish in the chart, and says, "That's the fish." The child may take the adult's hand, place it on his cheek, and "help" the adult in saying, "*Fish*," or "That's a *fish*." As he supposedly helps the adult, the adult is taking advantage of the game situation to help him. (Occasionally, the adult makes "a mistake" in order to give the child another opportunity of saying the word more intelligibly if possible, and of using expressions such as, "No, a flower," etc.)

SUGGESTION 4

Aim

To give the child more experience with numbers in relation to lipreading, speech, and auditory training.

Materials

Lightweight box with slot to represent a mail-box; peaked cap for child; ten or twelve envelopes; numerous, small, cardboard circles (penny size), preferably of a bright color.

Procedure

(1) Child puts on cap.

(2) Adult places cardboard circles on table, and gives the child an envelope. Adult takes an envelope, counts out two circles as the child watches, and puts *two* in the envelope. (If child has had sufficient number work, *three,* and then *four,* circles would be used in a like manner.) Time should be taken at this stage to show child what is expected of him.

(3) Child watches as adult says, *"Find two."* Child picks up two circles. Adult asks, *"How many* do you have?" Child counts the circles and says, "Two." Any assistance the child may need in getting the "right" number should be readily forthcoming and casual.

(4) Adult tells child to put *two* in the envelope.

(5) Child is given a second envelope. He is asked to find another number of circles, one, two, three or other number commensurate with his training and age.

(6) This procedure is followed until the child has put a specific number of circles in each of a number of envelopes.

(7) Throughout each activity, expressions such as "How many," "Count," "Put them in the envelope," "Put three in the envelope," etc., are used by the adult; and the child is encouraged and assisted in using spoken language corresponding to what he is doing.

186

(8) When a number of envelopes have been filled, the adult draws a number picture on each of the envelopes to indicate the number of circles in each, and places the envelopes on the table or on the floor.

(9) The adult points to each number picture and asks the child *"how many"* there are in that envelope. The child answers; and then opens the envelope and counts, to verify what he has said.

(10) The envelope flaps may be turned in rather than sealed, and the child would be asked to "mail *two* letters," *"three,"* etc.

(11) Small pieces of paper with the child's name on each might be placed in each envelope before "mailing."

SUGGESTION 5

Aim

To give the child practice in the use of consonants which have already been introduced to him in the words and sentences natural to general and specific situations. Tactile, visual, and auditory approaches would be used.

Materials

Large chart of stiff cardboard with substantial support at its back.

Several envelopes, one for each consonant to be practiced. Envelopes pasted, flap-side out, on cardboard. Consonant printed on flap of envelope.

Several pictures of familiar objects for each envelope, all pictures for each envelope showing objects whose names begin with the particular consonant printed on the outside of the envelope.

Procedure

(1) Pictures for practice of *b* would be taken from envelope marked *b*.

(2) Adult points to the picture of the *b*ow, places the child's hand on her cheek as she says "Bow," and "bububu-bow," and encourages child to repeat.

187

(3) Sentences such as, "What color is the bow?" "It's a red bow," etc., would be incorporated into the discussion that should revolve about each picture; and child would imitate as much of the spoken language as is possible for him.

(4) The picture of the bow is handed to the child and he, at the request of the adult, puts it in the *b* envelope.

(5) All pictures that belong in the *b* envelope would be treated in a like manner.

(6) Pictures in each of the other envelopes would be discussed, emphasis being upon the child's imitation of each word.

(7) Attention may be directed to the printed form on the envelope in accordance with the child's age and readiness. The three-year-old or younger, instead of being exposed to the printed form of the consonant on the envelope, would find on each envelope a picture of an object whose name begins with a particular consonant, and in each envelope, there would be other words beginning with the same consonant.

(8) Four- and five-year-olds, depending on the individual child, may have the printed word as well as the printed consonant on each envelope. Larger, hand-made envelopes may be necessary in this case, to accommodate words.

(9) Vowels as they occur in words may be practiced in a similar manner.

SUGGESTION 6:

Aim

To give the child practice in the use of color words in phrases and sentences.

Materials

Three-inch squares of cardboard each with a slit in center.
Pieces of colored ribbon, one drawn through the slit in each card and tied in bows.
Hearing aid.

Procedure

(1) Bows on cards placed before child, who wears earphones.

(2) Adult indicates each bow, talks about it as child watches, feels (hand on speaker's cheek), and listens. "That's a *blue bow*," "That's a *yellow bow*," "That's *purple bow*."

(3) With one hand on adult's cheek and other on his own cheek, child imitates each phrase and says it into the microphone.

(4) Adult says to child, "I'm going to tie a bow," and ties the blue bow. Then she says, "I tied a bow. A blue bow." Adult unties bow and says to the child, "You tie the blue bow." Child ties bow as well as he is able, and adult guides him in saying, "I tied a bow," and, "I tied a blue bow," as he watches, listens, and feels.

(5) Other bows would be used in a similar manner.

(6) As the child progresses, he may lipread, "Tie a blue bow"; "Tie a purple bow"; "Tie an orange bow"; etc.

(7) Throughout this exercise, emphasis is placed on the child's lipreading and his use of the color words in phrases and simple sentences. He should be permitted to "listen" to his own speech patterns as well as to the adult's, through the use of the hearing aid.

(8) The question form "What color" should be used whenever applicable.

SUGGESTION 7

Aim

To give the child practice in a play-way in the use of the adjectives *big* and *small,* in phrases and sentences, combining speech, lipreading, and auditory experience.

Materials

Several objects, bought or hand-made; for example, a big hat and a small hat, a big toy car and a small one, a big horn and a small one, a big wax apple and a small one, a big box and a small one.

Procedure

(1) The objects would be shown to the child one at a time: first a big one, then a small one; and he would be encouraged to imitate the phrase or sentence used by the adult.

(2) The objects would be placed in various positions about the room. Child goes with adult, and as each object is placed, the phrase would be repeated by adult and child.

(3) Adult and child return to table with a mirror near by.

(4) Adult says, "Find the *big* hat and bring it to me." Child gets hat and brings it to the adult. Adult says, "You have the *big* hat. Put it on." Then adult and child turn to the mirror and say in unison, or child after adult, "That's a *big* hat," or "A *big* hat." In this position, it is easy to speak near the child's ear as he watches in the mirror.

(5) Other objects would be used in a like manner.

(6) Adult must use the adjectives in irregular order, so that the child has to lipread, and cannot guess. That is, if a big object is asked for, then a small one, then big, small, etc., the child begins to reach for a big or small object automatically, without lipreading. The adult should ask for a small object, a big one, another big one, a small one, a small one, a small one, a big one, etc.

SUGGESTION 8

Aim

To make the child more familiar with the sequence of adjectives in phrases, using the visual, tactile, and auditory means. (Generally, this is for five-year-olds, although some four-year-olds have been ready for such specific work.)

Materials

A big, red hat; a small, red hat; a big, yellow hat; a small, yellow hat; a big, purple hat; a small, purple hat; etc.

Procedure

(1) The child would be asked to indicate the big hats, the small hats; would describe each as "big" or "small," with the adult's assistance if necessary; then he would place all the big hats together, and all the small ones together.

(2) The adult would say, indicating each group, "These are *big* hats, and these are *small* hats."

(3) The *big* hats would be discussed as to color, one by one. "That's a *blue* hat. It's *big* and it's *blue*. A *big, blue* hat." "That's a *red* hat. It's *big* and it's *red*. A *big, red* hat," etc. The child would watch the adult closely and he would repeat, "A *big, blue* hat," etc.

(4) A similar procedure would be followed, using the small hats of various colors.

(5) When the adult feels that the child has some idea of the differences in size or color or both, she would ask, "Show me the *big, blue* hat," etc.

(6) The number of hats and number of colors are increased as the child grows in understanding of the situation and in lip-reading skills.

(7) Throughout the exercise, the child is encouraged to use the phrases himself as frequently as possible, to establish the idea of sequence and to help prevent the use of incorrect sequence, which frequently happens among deaf children.

(8) Question forms such as "How many," "What color," "Is it big," or "Is it small," should be employed as much as possible.

SUGGESTION 9

Aim

To improve the child's use and understanding of language revolving about animals. (Same idea for foods, transportation, etc.)

Materials

Toy animals; pictures of each, some static, some involving activity such as walking, eating, etc.

Procedure

(1) Place a few toy animals before the child.

(2) Adult talks about each and the child repeats its names.

(3) The adult asks the child to indicate each animal as she asks, "Where is the dog?" "Where is the horse?" etc.

(4) Adult asks child to find the corresponding animals on the wall chart and to tell her the names of them.

(5) The animals on the chart are discussed as follows: "What is the horse doing?" "The horse is running." "What is the dog doing?" "The dog is jumping," etc.

(6) The adult presents three large envelopes containing pictures of each animal, varying in size, color, action, etc. The picture of each animal is pasted on the outside of the envelope, and also, for the older preschool child, the corresponding printed word and initial consonant of that word.

(7) An envelope is handed to the child, and the adult asks, indicating the picture, "What's that?" Child replies, "A dog."

(8) The adult opens the envelope and asks the child to get a picture from it. The child pulls out another picture of a dog.

(9) The picture is discussed using as many of the following questions as possible: "What color is the dog?" "Is the dog big?" "What is the dog doing?" "Who is playing with the dog?" "What does the dog say?" "Show me the dog's tail?" "How many legs does the dog have?" The child is guided in an understanding of such questions and in answering them.

(10) Other animals would be discussed in a similar manner.

(11) The child should be able to use the hearing aid for a large part of this lesson, and to listen to his own voice as well as to the adult's.

SUGGESTION 10

Aim

To give the child further practice in the use of vowels as they occur in words, in isolated form, and in the printed form. (For five-year-olds.)

Materials

A large chart for the vowels to be practiced, showing the printed form, a word containing the vowel, and a picture to illustrate the word; for example:

o͞o	shoe	(picture of a shoe)
ī	pie	(picture of a pie)

Individual vowel cards, one vowel to a card, to correspond with those on the large chart.

Individual word cards, one word to a card, to correspond with printed words on large chart.

Hearing aid.

Procedure

(1) Chart is placed near the child. Adult asks child to find the picture of the shoe. Then child and adult say the word "shoe" into the microphone.

(2) Adult points to the vowel on the chart, places the child's hand on her cheek and says into the microphone, "o͞o-bo͞obo͞obo͞o." Child repeats. Then, "sho͞osho͞osho͞o," and child repeats. Then "shoe," and child repeats.

(3) Adult points to the chart, moving her hand from left to right, saying, "o͞o" (for the vowel), "shoe" (for the printed word), and "shoe" for the picture. Child repeats.

(4) Adult takes the separate vowel cards and word cards, and shows child how each is matched to the corresponding one on the chart.

(5) Individual cards placed on the table before the child.

(6) Adult points to the word *shoe* and asks the child what it says. The child says, "Shoe," into the microphone; then matches the word on the card to the corresponding word on the chart.

(7) The child matches the vowels in a similar manner.

(8) Child and adult repeat, "ōō, *shoe,* shoe," indicating vowel, word, and picture on the chart.

(9) A similar procedure using the other vowels and words on the chart would be followed.

(10) Charts similar to those shown in Figure 2 for consonants (see page 118) may be made for vowel practice, so that a complete chart is supplied for each vowel.

(11) This type of exercise gives the child a broader concept of sounds as they occur in words which he has become familiar with. Five-year-olds have learned to find a number of ōō words from a series of pictures, a number of ī words, etc. The printed forms should not be emphasized. In fact it is quite possible to carry out such an exercise without the use of printed forms. The adult is concerned mainly with lipreading and use of language.

CHAPTER 14

Developmental Activities
for Language Development

CREATIVE ACTIVITIES

The activities provided for through busy hands and colorful media offer many opportunities for expression, and for casual training in lipreading, speech, and language understanding. If the activities are to be effective with the deaf child, the materials provided and the methods followed should parallel those employed in the guidance of the hearing child; and adult guidance of the deaf child should obey the laws of child growth rather than of deafness.

The following activities are among those which might be used to advantage by parent or teacher: (1) Easel painting, (2) finger painting, (3) paper cutting, (4) paper tearing, (5) pasting, (6) weaving, (7) paper folding, (8) lacing, (9) mural painting, (10) painting on felt, (11) crayon on felt, (12) crayon on paper, (13) clay manipulation and modeling, (14) construction with wood, (15) painting fences and large surfaces with large brush and water, (16) modeling houses and roads in sand, (17) building with blocks and planks, (18) visits to art centers, (19) excursions to see and appreciate the beauty of nature, as in flowers, the sky, trees, rain, pools of water, reflections in the water, etc., (20) room arrangement, flower arrangement, arrangement of toys on shelves.

Among the necessary materials and equipment for such activities are the following items: tables and chairs of right sizes for the respective children; easels of suitable height, and preferably adjustable; oilcloth covers for tables and easels; washable linoleum on floors; paint brushes with short thick handles and thick brushes; easel paper; crayons; pastels; drawing paper; pieces of felt, large and small; finger paint; finger painting paper; paint containers; water; painter's brushes for painting large surfaces with water; aprons; plasticine; clay; clay boards; clay pot; paste; small, blunt scissors; construction paper of various weights and colors; hammers and nails; planks of various sizes; sticks; log and chain; blocks of various sizes; folding and cutting paper; weaving paper; sewing cards and laces; sandbox and sand; materials for sewing and cutting.

In the presentation of materials for original and creative expression, the adult must remember the levels of development on which the child thinks and feels in regard to what he is doing. The child's efforts, pleasure, and interest in a specific activity are more important than the finished article. His use of the various materials gradually develops along the usual channels until he shows a conscious effort to create a definite form, although it may be at first unrecognizable to the adult and only later recognizable.[14]

This development is retarded if demands are made of the child to draw "this or that," to hurry, or if the adult interferes to do the child's work for him. Whatever contribution the child makes is acceptable, whether it is merely a heap of pounded clay or a mass of one color on a sheet of easel paper.[27] His *efforts* are worth-while, and the adult desires the child's voluntary expression entirely free of direct, adult influence. The principles of free expression should predominate.[21] (Plate XXIII)

The adult who is guiding the child in expressive activities must remember that the child's world is not the same as the adult's. His drawings, paintings, modeling, in the earliest years are not

PLATE XXIII.—Deaf children at indoor play in Nursery School.

recognizable, in most cases, to the adult. As his attempts take on a more "realistic" form, they are still out of proportion to the adult. To the child, that is not important; it is not out of proportion to him. If he draws a huge head on a miniature body, he probably sees it that way. To him, expression may seem to come from the face of a person, and is therefore more important than any other part of the body. He is concerned with expression as related to himself; and adult interference can be very frustrating for him. Freedom in such activities helps him to bridge the gap between his world and the adult's. The child is primarily concerned with the act as part of *himself* and *his* life.[220]

It is quite possible to follow these principles and make use of intervals here and there to talk to the child. The error made by so many people, especially over-conscientious parents, is that of "leaping at the child" when an opportunity to talk arises, and of destroying the value of the activity and the opportunity for language growth by making the whole situation unpleasant and annoying.[177] Then, there are those persons at the other extreme who, feeling that there is too much emphasis placed on communication, don't talk to the child at any time during the activity. Both groups are making the error of placing too much emphasis on the deafness; they talk too much in the situation, or not at all; and they forget that they are guiding *children*. No one should become so far removed from normal children that her guidance of the deaf child *as a child* is warped into taking some other direction. Teachers and parents of deaf children should take time regularly to stand back and "take stock" of their own actions, and ask themselves, "Do I talk too much in the 'wrong' situations?" and "Do I miss opportunities for talking to the child when it could be done easily for him and me?" "Do I really feel that these creative activities are valuable, or am I too concerned about making them one more means for attaining what *I* want for this child—speech?"

In all probability, if the adult is honest with herself, she will find that she does err in some way and can make the training better. If she is sincerely interested in the child's progress, she will continue to make every attempt to improve her methods before it is too late.

The adult never gestures to the deaf child when it is possible and plausible to talk. The preparation for each activity would include such expressions as, "Get your apron"; "The red paint is on the shelf"; "What color do you want?"; "John has the blue paint"; "Here is your brush"; "Let's wash our hands"; etc. When such expressions are used each day for a number of months, the child gradually learns to recognize the suggestion, the statement, the question, in association with the specific situation.

The three-year-old will show very few signs of proficiency in lipreading such phrases. He is still primarily concerned with expression and more expression. However, without special emphasis or imposition from the adult, a certain amount of "absorption" of language forms as related to himself and his interests is taking place.

Most three-year-olds cover pages quickly with paint, and want one page after another. The child may want to use just one color to a page, although he often begins to use more than one and intermixes them. When the colors are given to him, the adult might name them as they are placed in the box-shelf on the easel. When the painting period is over, the pages might be hung on a line to dry, and, later, be pinned on the wall. The adult might count the pages for the child, and, although number is irrelevant to the basic value of this activity, if the child is willing to give any attention to the situation, he may derive some value and some pleasure from watching the adult count his "works of art."

The three-year-old is concerned with his achievement as related to himself, and often indicates that he has made this or that, tapping his chest as he points to the finished pages. The adult follows up such actions with, "Yes, you made that, John. This is yours, too. This is a blue one, and this is a red one. I like them very much."

Some three-year-olds will make objects of clay and paint them. They may not be recognizable to the adult, but the child may attempt to name them by showing the adult a picture or an object in the room which it is meant to represent. The adult accepts what he has done, and makes no effort to change the form. She does, however, give the child the name of the object.

The little child sometimes enjoys having an adult sit with him and work with the clay. Even when the adult does this, the model should be well within the comprehension of the child, and should not be left in front of him alone to copy. He may learn something from watching the adult at work, but he should be permitted to take from the model what *he* desires, what *he* understands, and what *he* can do.

Throughout these activities, the three-year-old seldom reflects in speech and lipreading the language that has accompanied the activities. However, the value of both the activity and the language is revealed more clearly at the four-year level.

The three-year-old who has had experience with such activities —painting freely with brush and fingers,[186] learning to build with and balance blocks, manipulating and pounding clay until a form results, etc.—emerges as a four-year-old who is unafraid to tackle materials and media, who feels successful in his attempts, and is more persistent in working through a problem. He should have no fears of putting his fingers into clay and paint, nor of "getting dirty"; and his improved muscular coordination and emotional stability help him to be neater and more proficient in handling materials. His progress has been a result of free expression, of experience, and observation; *not* of adult demands for neatness, cleanliness, and specific results.

The child who reaches the age of four years with *fears* about getting his hands soiled needs attention, and his parents need advice. It is indeed a very sad sight to watch a young child painfully struggling to stay within lines, to remain "clean" instead of plunging into an activity with sheer enjoyment. There are parents who point with pride to their children who "insist" upon being clean all the time, who cry if a spot of color accidentally finds its way to a part of the page beyond the "working area." Unfortunately, the insistence and the cry did not originate with the child, but with the parent, and probably in situations entirely removed from creative activities. The parent cannot expect the child to express himself creatively at full capacity if emphasis is placed first on cleanliness by adult standards, not only in the activity situation but in other more basic situations, such as toilet training and eating habits, etc.

It has been stated earlier in the text that developmental activities may be a means of revealing problems as well as of solving them, and the earlier these problems are revealed, the sooner they may be solved by the adult, the teacher, the psychologist.[127]

The growing maturity of the relatively well-adjusted four-year-old offers many more opportunities for language growth and for a wider variety of activities.[162] The child grows ever more capable of producing from a number of media a form that *resembles* a "real" object or person. Often, he voluntarily tells the adult what he has created. He may nail a piece of cloth to a stick, and call the result a flag. He may draw a face with a crayon, and indicate that it represents his playmate or one of his parents. He may use the paint and brush for the portrait of a favorite animal, or he may model a favorite toy from clay. When the child brings his achievement to the adult to tell her what it is, she gives him the appropriate language, encouraging the child to imitate her while she endeavors to share his feeling of pride and achievement regarding the particular object.

After drawing a face, or a figure with a predominant face, the deaf four-year-old has used words such as *eye, nose, mouth,* etc. The adult may respond with, "Yes, that's an eye. There are two eyes. You have two eyes," etc. If the child has drawn, painted, or constructed a car from blocks, and brings the adult's attention to it, adult and child may talk about its color, the fact that Daddy has a car, etc.

The experience of the child at this age usually causes him to prefer a color or colors, and he learns to ask for the specific colors. Although the adult should not spend time here on articulation, she does encourage the child to ask for any color, using appropriate language. If the child has derived pleasure and satisfaction from the activities, he begins to use the language of the activities more spontaneously and more frequently.

Some four-year-olds have exhibited their first conscious awareness of printed forms during creative activities. Occasionally, in the midst of a maze of lines and colors, letters have appeared; and the child has indicated, not only that he did it, but that the letter or letters refer to him. In one case, the child printed M in a corner of a page, and pointed to himself. His name began with M, and of the whole word which he had seen printed on his drawings each day, that letter stood out. He recognized a connection between himself and the finished work, and between the marks on the paper (printed by the adult) and himself.

When the child printed M on the paper with his paint brush, the adult accepted the attempt with sincere approval, even though the letter was large and asymmetrical. She showed him a card with his name printed on it, said his name; and the child repeated it. The child pointed to the M he had printed and to the one at the beginning of his name on the card. No attempt was made to improve upon the child's contribution at this time. It remained on the front of the page as the sole indication of possession. Within a few months following, the child was printing his whole first name with the paint brush, so that it was recognizable, if not "perfect," with every letter in correct sequence, without copying, and without having been "taught" to print. Still later, but at the four-year-level, he also carved his name after a fashion in clay, with his finger or with a stick.

Four-year-olds enjoy work with felt. Crayons, paints, and pastels may be used effectively on felt. The pieces of felt should vary in size for experience in drawing on small and large surfaces, and for practice of the terms, *big* and *small*.

Paper work is also an enjoyable experience. The child learns to produce various shapes through folding, cutting, and tearing paper. The use of scissors should not be required until the small muscle coordination is sufficiently developed to manage manipulation of scissors and paper. The child might use them to cut paper at random, and *much later* he may be able to attempt cutting along lines to produce specific shapes.

Paper work involves intelligent adult guidance to prevent, in so far as it is possible, any frustration or a feeling of loss on the part of the child for having mutilated a piece of paper. The five-year-old handles scissors and paper much more efficiently than does the four-year-old. The younger child's evident interest in scissors and in cutting paper does not mean that he can use scissors and paper with the skill of an older child. Many four-year-olds tend to "try anything" and to show off their skills in as many ways as possible. This can be either advantageous or problematical for the child, depending to a large degree on the guidance of the adult.

The adult has to manage the activities in such a way that they are challenging and interesting but not potentially frustrating, beyond the four-year-old's capacity to adjust to possibly unacceptable or discouraging results. In woodworking, frustrating incidents can be overcome, partially at least, by the child's pounding out his feelings on the wood with a hammer; and very little damage is done to the finished article which has come to assume some importance for the child. However, in paper work, crushing and tearing in the face of frustration may satisfy an immediate feeling, but when the child views the results of his act, other feelings of frustration and failure may be aroused. Every child encounters frustrating experiences, which he must learn to face and overcome. However, there are situations which cause the destructive kind of frustration, neither necessary nor valuable from any viewpoint, and unfortunately, the activity situation has become too often the parade ground for such unhealthy developments. The adult who is guiding the child must be especially skilful in knowing what activities to present, how to guide the child, and when and where to step into the situation to support the child without weakening his sense of possession and achievement.[114]

The child of five is quite different from the four-year-old. The world has enlarged for him and he is more aware of it. He finds out that this broader and more interesting world makes more demands on him. He takes pride in his endeavors, and enjoys the sincere praise of adults. False praise he has learned to recognize, despise, and take advantage of; and if he has been the victim of this kind of adult response, his dissatisfaction may be reflected in his attitudes towards the achievements of other children.[19] The five-year-old who has been subjected in the earlier years to false praise, or bribes (there is little difference between the two), will have more difficulty in adjusting to the demands which his age place upon him. If he has been guided by adults who sincerely appreciate him and respect him, his adjustment to his world as a five-year-old will be easier.

The deaf child of five enjoys the activities which most children of kindergarten age enjoy.[221] There is a great need for creative endeavor at this level, as means of self-expression, emotional outlet, and language practice.[113]

The deaf child of five, who has had earlier nursery school training featuring equipment and materials for creative expression, usually lipreads the names of those materials and the equipment. He has learned to understand through lipreading the language involved in the getting and putting away of materials.

Five-year-olds who have had previous training should have little difficulty in following directions such as: "Billy, you may get the red paint and the yellow paint." "Jimmy, you may get the paint brushes." "Bobby, would you like to help me put the paper on the easels?" etc. If the child doesn't understand immediately, the sentence is repeated for him; and if he still fails to understand, he *is shown* what is meant, just as he was shown at earlier levels in other, simpler situations.

The five-year-old draws, paints, and constructs objects and forms that are recognizable, at least to him, and usually to the adult. He will try to name them spontaneously, or will ask the adult how to say the word or words he wants to use. There tends to be an interchange of ideas among deaf children at this level; and, in a group of deaf children participating in creative activities, *conversation* takes place among them.

The child at this age has little difficulty in thinking of something to draw, to paint, or construct. He has learned to bring his home, school, and other experiences to the easel, to the paper, to the clay, or to the woodworking corner. He is learning to express himself in terms of what has impressed him.[102]

The five-year-old frequently demonstrates his developed sense of color, his awareness of space and form, and his ability to use colors dramatically and with originality in creating forms and designs.[43] Some deaf children are interested in making designs using squares, circles, triangles, and other shapes, and in filling in each space with a particular color. Some fill in the spaces with favorite animals, objects, or people whom they can name.

In one instance where a group of five deaf children were participating in creative activities, three of them filled pages with very effective designs entirely of their own making. The teacher hung them on the wall, which was papered. One of the children immediately noticed a connection between the wallpaper design and the designs on the paintings. The teacher agreed with her observation, for the first time was able to give the word *wallpaper* to the children in a meaningful situation, and went on to show the children that there were also pretty designs in the floor linoleum. Before long, every child in the group had tried his hand at creating original wallpaper and linoleum designs. It was interesting also, to note that the designs of the linoleum and wallpaper of the room were not copied.

Group activity at the five-year-old level frequently stimulates best efforts and a maximum of enjoyment and application. The children often show enthusiasm over group projects, such as the painting of murals depicting their joint experiences—an excursion to the park, free play in the yard, a visit to the zoo, etc. The deaf child may participate in such group activity with other deaf children, or with hearing children.

One group of five-year-olds completed a mural illustrating the nursery school yard. Each child took responsibility for the part for which he had a preference and which he tended to do best. The one who liked to cover large surfaces with paint, and who managed in a "free and easy" way to get interesting effects with paint, did the sky and the ground. Another did the cutting; another the pasting; another the painting of small objects; and so on. The completed mural served not only as a room decoration, but as a means of demonstrating to the children the attractive results of group participation, and also as a source of language practice. Such questions as, "What is this?" "Who drew the swing?" "Who painted the sky?" "What color is it?" "Where is the sandbox?" were asked of the children. The children also enjoyed playing teacher in turn, and asking simple questions of one another regarding the mural.

Each child attains a different degree of skill in the various activities. One child may cut out materials and even use a needle with ease, while another might have great difficulty in managing such activities. One child may turn out a very good piece of woodwork with ease and speed; another of the same age may not get beyond hammering a nail into a board. One child may appear quite talented in painting, and show little skill or interest in paper folding. An attempt should be made to permit each child to do what he likes to do, at the same time that he is offered the opportunity of observing and participating in all other activities. This encourages the child to develop his special interest to the extent of his five-year-old possibilities, and to experience all other activities in some degree.

MUSIC AND RHYTHM

Music is a language. Rhythm is a language. Music and rhythm are both means of expression. This holds true for the deaf child as for the hearing; but music and rhythm serve an additional purpose for the deaf child. They serve as outstanding means of developing more natural speech.

What are some of the characteristics of the speech of the deaf that make it so different from that of the hearing? Inflection is frequently lacking; breathing is not regulated to the utterances of the speaker, so that the speech is less intelligible to the listener; rhythm in speech is broken; muscles are tense; tone is monotonous; pitch is often abnormally high or low; resonance is frequently lacking; and rate of speaking is often slow and laborious. Music and rhythmic exercises can help to prevent such characteristics to some extent, if applied consistently to various phases of the child's experience at the preschool stage.

Music may be incorporated into the lessons in auditory training, lipreading, speech, and creative activities. There should be a short period each day devoted to music and rhythmic exercises where they are the center of interest, and where the other phases of the training are secondary to them.[211]

The adult should have some definite objectives in mind when guiding little deaf children in musical games and rhythmic activities. Objectives and the program should coincide as closely as possible with those for the hearing child. The adult has to be quite realistic about the deaf child's limitations in relation to music, and must remember that certain developments will, of necessity, be slow. However, the development should be limited only by the deafness and capacities of the individual child, not by the adult's possible negative attitude towards music for the deaf child.

Exposure to music stimulates spontaneity, individually and with the group. It encourages the child to express his feelings of joy, dramatic action, creative expression, and individual interpretations. It aids the child in developing more graceful movements and motor skills. He develops a sense of rhythm which carries over into his speech, since muscles of the body, including the speech muscles, learn to move more rhythmically. Activity with music develops the relaxation which is so essential to good speech. The child has an opportunity to coordinate music and bodily movements with the voice in a relaxed, spontaneous manner, in a situation where no demands are placed upon him for better articulation. The adult hopes to increase the child's ability to change pitch for expression as the rhythm, timing, and expression change in the music.

The adult hopes to develop in the deaf child an interest in the activities related to music.[204] To attain this end, he must be introduced to music through familiar channels that include pleasant activities and freedom in movement and expression; and the adult, herself, must enjoy the situation. In the beginning, the adult finds herself adapting the rhythm of the music to the child's movements, rather than expecting the child to adapt his movements to the music. No technical approach nor specific responses are necessary. Freedom and originality are the keynotes of the music periods.

The little child, deaf or hearing, enjoys random movements. It may be patting clay, beating on a toy drum, putting pegs in a pegboard, rocking a doll's cradle, or drawing strokes on paper with a paintbrush or crayon. The adult, whenever possible, would play a selection in time to what the child is doing. Gradually, as the child becomes aware of the vibration and rhythm of the music, he begins to recognize a connection between what he is doing and the music which the adult is playing. Eventually, he notices that each time he pats the clay, he "feels" a "beat" from the piano.

Sometimes, if the teacher and the parent, or two parents, are present, one may play the piano while the other guides the child. The following simple exercise worked out very effectively in a situation where parent and teacher were working together in the child's training program. While the teacher played the piano, parent and child stood beside the piano with a pegboard on top of the piano in front of them. The child was leaning on the piano while the parent placed one hand on it, and with the other hand took pegs out of the board in time to the music. The child had a choice of taking out some pegs or of just watching. In this case, he watched. After a few sessions, he began to do what the parent was doing. The parent began at one end of the board, and the child began at the other end, which was closer to him. Part of the rhythm of his movements was, of course, an echo of the parent's movements. This was considered quite acceptable and worthy of approval. The child was guided in keeping time to the music without having any adult pressure placed upon him to do so. Gradually, he became aware of the beat of the music in direct relation to his own movements, and he was able to do the exercise himself before his fourth birthday.

Some four-year-olds, who have had previous training with music, learn to do similar exercises combining them with speech play; for example, saying, "pum, pum, pum," in time to their movements and to the music.

It must be kept in mind that specific exercises related to music, if unwisely managed, are not helpful. In no one exercise should the child be *expected* to keep time to music.[151] He will learn to do it after a while, following the steps leading up to it which involve simple activities of interest to him. The most important preliminary is that the adult *take the music to the child* in a way that he can understand. Each child differs from others in coordination and individual interests, and his ability to "understand" what the adult is trying to put across to him is at a minimum. The young child is much more interested in experimenting with his body, in amusing himself with sounds *he* makes and feels, than he is in "following directions."

The young deaf child should have the opportunity of seeing various musical instruments, of touching them and feeling the vibration and rhythm as they are played. The adult may find that the child is developing an interest in the piano and the book of music, and in so far as it is possible he should be given a chance to understand the connection between the notes and the playing, the notes and singing.

The child of nursery and kindergarten years enjoys movements such as running, jumping, falling, and hopping. Enjoyable, rhythmic exercises involving such actions might be carried out in conjunction with stories, excursions, and animal pictures. The adult might play a selection that would suit the tempo and mode of walking of a particular animal. The elephant, for example, is pictured with big, heavy feet, and most children have seen a live one at the zoo. The accompanying music might be slow and emphatic, and the child might imitate the walk of the elephant in time to the music. One five-year-old who had been to the zoo many times and had liked the elephant, would thump along for a few steps in time to the music, then would stand on his "hind" legs and stamp heavily on the spot, then go on walking for a few more steps. Such spontaneous interpretations are encouraged. even though they aren't always as realistic as the adult might think they should be.

The child may learn the concepts *soft* and *loud, quiet* and *noisy,* through music. The adult might show the child a picture of a baby sleeping, and show him how we tiptoe, or walk quietly, to quiet music.

Some activity with music may follow the storytelling period. After the story of "The Three Bears," the child may touch the piano and the adult's cheek or throat, as he senses the high squeal of the little bear, the soft voice of the mother bear, and the low growl of the father bear, as suggested by chords on the piano.

Some five-year-olds like to use rhythm band instruments. If they have had earlier experiences with music, they may be able to keep relatively good time with the instruments and to coordinate the voice with the movements involved. Where there is a group of deaf children, the adult may find that among five-year-olds there are those who like to conduct and who should have the experience. Some five-year-olds have learned to check the rhythm of the other children, although this is neither required nor expected.

Deaf children discover that interesting stories may be sung. Deaf children, after having listened to the story of "Mary Had a Little Lamb," like to watch, clap, and sing with the adult as she plays the piano. The preschool child's desire for repetition—to listen to the same song over and over, and to play the same music game over and over—simplifies the adult's task of guiding him and provides naturally for the repetition necessary to language development, as well as for enjoyment and developmental growth.

Music for three- and four-year-olds should be brought to them through what they happen to be doing, whereas the five-year-old often has ideas to contribute, and has less difficulty in coordinating movements, music, and voice. The five-year-old deaf child has learned to "sing" a word at different pitches, for example, "Run, run, run,"—the first high, the second medium, the third low.

Five-year-olds who have had previous training have learned to march to music, to say sentences to music, to make up dances, to participate in rhythm bands, and to maintain a certain rhythm throughout a selection.[110]

In spite of the trained five-year-old's growing ability to understand music in relation to other activities, the adult must bear in mind that even at this age the child is still limited, due to his deafness and his age; and that *technical* training should be at a minimum. The idea of the music program is to encourage spontaneity, free use of the voice in relation to music and activity, free use of the body, and emotional expression.

Many deaf children have used a better inflected speech in spontaneous situations after exercises with music than from specific speech instruction, although the articulation may not have been as good. However, since pitch and breathing are so important to more normal speech for the deaf child, and since he has to breathe more freely while actively engaged in a rhythmic exercise which he enjoys for enjoyment's sake, it is possible that his use of voice in such situations could effect a better coordination of speech and breathing. Young deaf children have developed better speech as a result of alternating and correlating the specific speech lesson and the spontaneous, free use of voice in the music and rhythmic exercises.

Neither teacher nor parent should expect the deaf child to become a musician or a singer; but they should like to see him develop an understanding of the role of music in society, and a feeling that he may join in with a singing group if he wishes to do so. He may be guided towards recognizing his limitations, but at the same time will feel less "different." Music will be one thing that he cannot manage as well as he does other things, and in that respect he is not unlike many hearing people. Music should not be something remote and unknown to him. The self-confidence and originality he developed through music and rhythmic activities as a child will supplement the confidence, assurance, and originality in other fields, in which he has become skilled. Music and rhythm help to improve speech and language; but most importantly, they help the child in socialization.[207]

BOOKS, DRAMATIZATIONS, AND EXCURSIONS

The child learns through experience, and one way of ensuring his present and future enjoyment of living is to establish a pleasant familiarity with books. He must be permitted to spend time

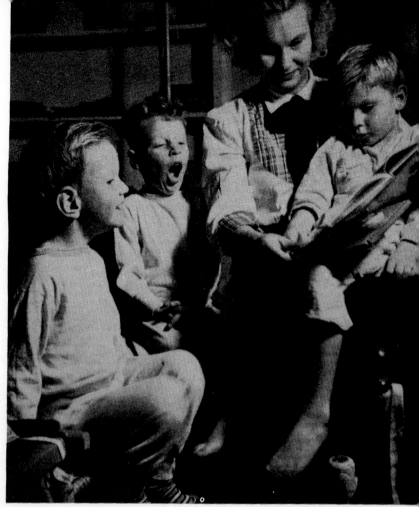

Photo by Ross Madden   *Courtesy John Tracy Clinic*

PLATE XXIV.—Story telling in Nursery School before napping.

in the company of books, to look through them, to share and exchange them with his friends, and to bring them to adults for explanation and mutual enjoyment. This kind of experience helps him in learning to turn to a book for the definite purpose of obtaining information, or for pastime, and for a broadening of his experiences. He should be exposed to books in as many situations as possible, as a beginning step in reading readiness, even before he is aware of printed words or their significance. (Plate XXIV)

Dramatization and excursions help to maintain and stimulate interest in books. The adult allows the child to become familiar with certain books. Then she tells him a story from one, showing pictures of each episode. The child learns to live through these experiences and to understand them more thoroughly by imitating the actions illustrated.

The child learns to recognize similar experiences and ideas in other books and stories, and to tie up his own experiences with what he sees in the books, what he has dramatized, and what he has seen on the lips of the storyteller.

Excursions are a necessity in the development of the child. The adult cannot take for granted that the child will understand what is seen in a picture if he has not had an experience of the real thing. This need is especially acute in the young deaf child whose lack of language understanding makes many verbal explanations futile. Along with the verbal explanations, he has to see or experience the situation in reality, before the adult can be sure that he understands it through pictures and stories. After having seen a series of pictures of a particular place or activity, the real situation which he encounters later will mean something to him; but the books and the stories have more meaning for him if he has already had similar, real experiences.

Every nursery school and home should have a library corner for the deaf child. Tables and chairs should be comfortable, and the height of the book cases or shelves should be suitable.

Cushions and rugs sometimes add to the child's enjoyment of and interest in using the corner. A collection of plants, insects, and other objects that might be mentioned or pictured in the books, stimulates the child's interest in books and in exploration.

Books in the library should be suitable to the child's age-level and individual interests, and should be well illustrated. If the child has made any books, they should be included in the library. The books should be easy to handle, in strong attractive bindings, on good quality, unglazed paper, and by authors who offer something worth-while to a child. If possible, there should be more than one book for each story. For example, "The Three Bears" is published in several different editions, each telling the same story, but in different language and with different pictures that put it across.

Experiences with books, dramatizations, and excursions develop interests in new experiences, in vocabulary building and language, and help in developing character.[34]

OTHER ACTIVITIES

The young deaf child, in nursery school and at home, learns many language concepts as he prepares for and participates in routine activities such as eating, resting, toileting, free play, and exploring various parts of the building such as the kitchen, the living room, or the sitting rooms, the offices, etc. The conversations in conjunction with such activities are casual, and the child learns to understand the language concepts through association with real routines that go on every day.

Washing and toileting situations provide many opportunities for exposure to casual language. The child in nursery school and, if he has brothers and sisters, in his home often has to wait his turn; and, often, one child stands by and watches while another washes his hands. Occasionally, the adult may talk to the child who is waiting. "Johnny is washing his hands. When he has finished, you will wash yours. Dry your hands, Johnny. Billy is going to wash his hands now."

The child begins to notice that the adult cleans the washbowl after he has washed, and often takes responsibility for doing this himself.

Every deaf child should have some kitchen experience, for purposes of preventing many dangerous habits that the curious, inexperienced child may develop, of overcoming "fussy" eating habits, and of adding to his experiences. The feeling of accomplishment, of being important and "grown-up," makes the child's role in the kitchen very important to his total development. The smelling, tasting, feeling, and seeing which the child experiences in the kitchen activities are an essential part of his sense training.

The adult who takes the child into the kitchen must realize that there may be some waste, many mistakes, and even accidents; but in consideration of the value of the experiences, a broken dish or some spilled milk should not eliminate the "kitchen program."

The preschool deaf child has learned to prepare and cook vegetables, to make cookies, toast, salads, and other simple dishes under unforced, well-planned guidance. He may learn the names of the utensils, and their uses. He learns to understand such expressions as, "Get the flour," "Fill the cup," "Put the flour in the bowl," etc. He learns how and when the stove is used. Children who have had their curiosity regarding the use of stoves and matches satisfied are less likely to indulge in dangerous activities with stoves, burners, matches, etc.

In nursery school, four- and five-year-olds have made food dishes in groups. The children stood in a semicircle behind their tables, each with his or her set of utensils and ingredients, and as the teacher gave instructions, the children watched, lipread, and performed. The teacher had her own utensils and ingredients before her to show the children what she meant as she talked. Lipreading and activity were coordinated.

The casual conversations that take place in the midst of developmental activities are essential since they are usually composed of the language of everyday living. They are usually effective since the activity holds the center of interest rather than the lipreading or speech.

The adult who is guiding the young deaf child will not underestimate the value of developmental activities, and will use them to broaden the child's experiences, his understanding, and his means of expressing himself.

PART 3

The Nursery School
for Deaf Children
and Parent Education

CHAPTER 15

The School— Introduction

The center which provides nursery school training for deaf children and includes parent education has become widely accepted
as a very effective means of putting the deaf child into communication with his world, and enabling him at the same time to
make his necessary social and personal adjustments.

In time, research will prove a great deal which for the present
must be accepted or rejected on a more subjective basis. Where
nursery schools for deaf children and parent education programs
have been in operation, the majority of the parents and educators involved have been in agreement regarding certain ob-
servations, results, and indications.

Many more individual deaf children have developed and begun to *use* language and speech skills *before* entering Grade I
of the School for the Deaf. The personal and social adjustments
of the child have become more fully adequate through the understanding of the trained parent. Parent participation in the deaf
child's total development has eliminated many of the "differences" that have set apart the deaf child from the hearing child.
The progress in the grades has been accelerated wherever the
school curriculum and philosophy provided for the individual
child to advance as quickly as he was able. The educated parent
has been able to supplement the training of the grade teacher,
and to educate the community. There have been many indications that the early development of social, intellectual, and motor

221

skills, through nursery school training and parent education, will make higher education (high school and college) possible for many more deaf individuals.

Besides providing for guidance of the parent in speech and language development and child development, the parent education program also offers the educator an opportunity to clarify certain publicity and principles which could be harmful if accepted as "absolutes" without question.[215]

For example, there is a theory that severely deaf children who have had preschool training should attend hearing classes, rather than go to a class for the deaf. Parents should understand that even the best preschool training does not eliminate the deaf child's need for further language training and, in most cases, the schools for hearing children are not adequately equipped to cope with such special language needs.

Many other problems related to the education of the deaf may be revealed through nursery school and parent education. The discovery of problems is important. Adequate solutions may not develop quickly, and there is indeed some danger in "quick" solutions. Nevertheless, the recognition and the statement of problems are a contribution.

The education of the deaf still remains one of the most challenging fields. There is much yet to be explored, to be discovered and resolved. Further studies in the nursery school education of deaf children and in parent education should produce, in time, new ways to effect more satisfying and satisfactory guidance of the deaf child.

A belief in giving language and speech to the deaf child, a belief in the child and in his parents, are important and must be accompanied by constructive measures that combine whatever of the "old" and of the "new" is workable and valuable in the light of the child's possibilities.

CHAPTER 16

Design for Nursery School and Parent Education

A. SPACE AND EQUIPMENT

1. *Nursery Quarters* (Indoors)

   A playroom.

   A bathroom.

   A dining room and a kitchen are necessary if the children remain through the lunch hour.

   (a) Rooms must be adequate as to space, ventilation, safety, and cleanliness.

   (b) Tables, chairs, shelves, toilets, basins, cots, etc., of a size suitable to the various age-levels and individual children.

   (c) Individual lockers.

   (d) Storage space.

   (e) Educational toys, books, creative materials, blocks, etc.

   Note—Where a cold climate does not permit a maximum of outdoor play, the indoor play area must be large enough to include extra equipment.

2. *Room for Special Training*

   (a) Adjacent to indoor and outdoor play areas.

   (b) As quiet as possible.

   (c) One-way vision screen and outer observation corridor.

   (d) *Essential Equipment:*

       i) Group hearing aid, or table model aid, or both.

       ii) Phonograph and recordings.

223

      iii) A mirror.

      iv) Sense training materials.

      v) Paper materials for lipreading and speech charts.

      vi) Shelves and storage space.

      vii) Chairs and table.

  (e) *Other Equipment:*

      i) A recording machine.

      ii) A piano.

3. *LECTURE ROOM* for Parents' Classes

4. *Office Space* and *Staff Quarters*

  Note—One room may serve a number of purposes, if overlapping of schedules can be prevented. The children's quarters should *not* be used for other purposes.

5. *OUTDOOR SPACE AND EQUIPMENT*

  (a) Large enough to provide for free play and play equipment.

  (b) Well-fenced. (This reduces the number of persons needed for adequate supervision of the children.)

  (c) Ladders, jungle gym, slides, swings, sand-box, crates, planks, boxes.

  (d) Storage.

B. STAFF

1. *Trained Teacher of the Deaf,* preferably one experienced in work with young deaf children and their parents.

2. *Trained Nursery School Teacher.*

3. *Assistants:* students, parents.

4. Some provision must be made for the daily health inspection of the children. A suitable arrangement is usually worked out with the public health nurse in the district.

5. A *Consulting Otologist* and a *Hearing Consultant* should be easily accessible.

6. A Qualified *Psychologist.*

7. A *Cook,* if the children remain through the lunch hour.

8. *Secretarial Assistance.*
9. *A Cleaning Woman.*
10. *A Director,* who, in the event of a very small organization, might be the *Teacher of the Deaf.* If the organization demands a full-time director, it is preferable that the individual be one trained in the education of the deaf, and in nursery school procedures.

C. SCHEDULE FOR CHILDREN IN NURSERY SCHOOL

1. Attendance from 9 a.m. to 3 p.m. four days a week.

or

2. Attendance from 9 a.m. to 12 noon, five days a week.
3. Attendance from 9 a.m. to 12 noon for two- and three-year-olds, five days a week;

and

from 2:30 to 5 p.m. for four- and five-year-olds, five days a week.

Note—Schedules #2 and #3 eliminate the need for a cook, the setting up of nutritional diets, a kitchen and kitchen equipment. They also eliminate some valuable opportunities such as the parents' observation of the children during afternoon naps, during lunches.

Schedule #3 is effective where there is a large number of children and where space and supervisory staff are limited.

Where Schedule #1 is in operation, the fifth day of the week might be set up as a "Clinic Day" to meet the needs of those parents and deaf children who, for very real reasons, are unable to attend a regular program.

Where Schedule #2 is in operation, the afternoons might be devoted to these extra cases.

4. Each day, full day, or half day attendance includes for each child:

(a) a period of individual instruction in language, speech lipreading, auditory training, and sense training;

225

(b) a period of free play;

(c) a period of creative and expressive activities;

(d) a rest, or nap period;

(e) mid-morning "snack" of juice and crackers.

D. SCHEDULE FOR PARENTS

1. One day a week to observe and participate in all phases of the child's training in nursery school.

2. One day a week to attend parents' classes in speech and language development, in child development, and in psychological guidance.

3. Responsibility for bringing the child to school on time, and of taking him home promptly at the closing hour.

4. Other responsibilities regarding sheets, towels, aprons, etc., for the child in nursery school.

5. Arrangements are made with the teacher in charge regarding individual consultations. Consultations regarding the child's progress should be held each week on the parent's observation day.

6. Responsibility of keeping records under the guidance and supervision of the teacher or teachers, and of submitting them on a weekly basis on the observation day.

7. The schedule for parents should be planned so that one or more parents observe and participate each day in nursery school, except on the day set aside for parents' classes which all the parents should attend.

8. Arrangements for individual consultations with the psychologist, when these are advisable, would be planned by the psychologist in accordance with the particular parent's schedule and needs.

E. PARENTS' CLASSES

(a) The weekly classes for the parents of deaf children should include:

      i) necessary information regarding the problems and the education of the deaf child;

      ii) demonstrations with the children from nursery school putting into practice the basic principles;

      iii) a discussion period during which the parents ask questions, comment, and make suggestions regarding i) and ii).

(b) All principles and practices in these classes should coincide with the principles and practices of the nursery school, and should be pertinent to home training and guidance.

(c) Information regarding speech and language development, and child development, should be correlated.

F. MAJOR TOPICS IN SPEECH AND LANGUAGE DEVELOPMENT

1. Philosophy and aims of a training program for young deaf children and their parents.
2. Determining what aspects of speech are essential in consideration of the *whole* child.
3. Relationship between speech and language.
4. Speech development in hearing children and in deaf children; where and how these deviate; means of decreasing the degree of deviation.
5. The speech mechanism, and how emotions and emotional problems may affect the functioning of this mechanism.
6. The auditory mechanism and causes of deafness.
7. Methods of training—visual, tactile, auditory, rhythmic, and kinesthetic.
8. Phonetic alphabet; Northampton Charts; diacritical markings; how and when each may be used in the training of the child.
9. Babbling and speech play.
10. Steps in speech teaching.
11. Lipreading—difficulties, aids, methods.

12. Sense training in the life of the child.
13. Audiometric testing. Testing the hearing of young deaf children. Assisting parents in interpreting audiograms and other test results.
14. Auditory training. Procedures, values, what the parent can do.
15. Formation and development of consonant sounds.
16. Formation and development of vowel sounds.
17. Language and the important role of the parent. Relation to speech, lipreading, reading, social adjustment, and home environment.
18. Reading readiness and its relation to other phases of learning.
19. Creative activities; their relation to speech and language development and to personality development.
20. Display and discussion of materials and equipment for nursery school and home training.
21. Discussion of reading materials for parents. Discussion of reading assignments for parents. Discussion of completed reading assignments.
22. Guidance in keeping and using records.
23. Guidance in choosing a school for the child. The parent must make the choice.
24. Publicity regarding the education of the young deaf child, and assistance in evaluating it.
25. The parent's responsibility to the community.

G. MAJOR TOPICS IN CHILD DEVELOPMENT

1. Guidance of the child in the home and in the nursery school should be based on the child's needs as an individual.
2. The role of the parent; the role of the teacher. Differences and similarities. The need for cooperation and consistency.
3. The fundamental needs of the child: (a) love and acceptance; (b) food and drink; (c) elimination; (d) rest and sleep;

(e) shelter.
4. Toileting.
5. Washing.
6. Eating.
7. Sleeping.
8. Dressing, undressing, care of clothing.
9. Intellectual, physical, social, and emotional development of the child at the various age-levels.
10. Discipline: ways and means of disciplining; most effective means; difference between permissiveness, indulgence, indifference, and authoritarianism;
11. Parent-child, teacher-child, child-child relationships.

Note—The order of consideration of the topics listed above will depend on the needs of the group and the individual, and on the period of time the parent will remain in training. There is a constant overlapping and correlation of subjects throughout the training program.

The responsibility of guiding the parents in an understanding of the problems of deafness and in the guidance of their children is a demanding one for the teacher. Some parents assimilate information and adjust to the "teaching situations" much more rapidly than others. The teacher must anticipate the needs and capabilities of the individual parent in relation to such situations. Through the cooperative efforts of the teacher and the psychologist, the parent should be guided and supported in achieving adequate independence of teacher and psychologist. The foregoing statement is not meant to imply that all parents should become independent of educators; there must always be some interdependence between the two.

The desired "independence" of the parent implies, first, acceptance of responsibility for the child "as a whole." Observation of the children in all situations, of the teacher and other parents at work with the children, and eventually, participation in the various guidance situations, promote the parent's self-assurance, and decrease the dependence upon the teacher. Failure to achieve adequate independence could result in the parent's placing the entire responsibility of guiding the child upon the teacher and the nursery school, and so would defeat the whole purpose of the program for parent and child.

The teacher is bound to offer information and intelligent guidance. The parent must be willing to learn and to grow, and to assume responsibility for guiding the child to oral communication and personal adjustment to the world in which he must live.

REFERENCES

(See Bibliography, page 247.)

11, 12, 24, 30, 32, 37, 38, 39, 41, 42, 48, 54, 55, 59, 66, 67, 68, 77, 80, 92, 99, 105, 106, 107, 108, 109, 115, 126, 130, 131, 132, 140, 142, 143, 144, 148, 150, 152, 157, 158, 162, 165, 167, 170, 178, 179, 180, 181, 182, 187, 188, 190, 191, 196, 198, 199, 202, 204, 209.

CHAPTER 17

Record Forms

WEEKLY REPORT TO THE PARENT (1)

*no.*_____

*date*_____

Child_____Teacher_____

SENSE TRAINING

1. *Sense of Sight* (Matching-Color-Shape-Memory)
2. *Sense of Touch*

SPEECH AND SPEECH PREPARATION

1. *Babbling, speech play,* etc.
2. *Consonants, vowels, combinations*
3. *Words, phrases, sentences*
    Note *a. degree of intelligibility under instruction*
    b. attempts at spontaneous speech and intelligibility
4. *Characteristic Voice Quality and Intensity*
5. *Difficulties*
6. *Auditory Training* (Activity-Response)
7. *Piano* (Rhythm-Pitch-Inflection-Accent)
8. *Attitude*

Weekly Report to the Parent (2)

no._____

date_____

LIPREADING AND LANGUAGE

1. *Nouns* (Objects-Pictures)
2. *Commands* (Action verbs)
3. *Color*
4. *Number*
5. *Verbs*
6. *Other Adjectives*
7. *Adverbs*
8. *Pronouns*
9. *Prepositions*
10. *Conjunctions*
11. *Sentences, phrases, expressions*
12. *Questions, question forms* (Answers)
13. *Stories, rhymes, jingles*

REMARKS—RE GENERAL AND SPECIFIC LIPREADING OF THE CHILD—RE ATTITUDE OF CHILD TOWARDS LIPREADING

Report on Child and Parent

no._____

date_____

This is not given to the parent, but is kept on file with a duplicate of the report given to the parent)

PARENT'S WEEKLY REPORT TO THE TEACHER (1)

no._____

date_____

Child _____ Parent _____

SENSE TRAINING

1. *Sense of Sight* (Matching-Color-Shape-Memory)
2. *Sense of Touch*

SPEECH AND SPEECH PREPARATION

1. *Babbling, speech play,* etc.
2. *Words, phrases, sentences, expressions* (Intelligible, unin telligible, spontaneous, through imitation)
3. *Auditory Training* (Activity-Response)

_____

PARENT'S WEEKLY REPORT (2)

no._____

date_____

LIPREADING AND LANGUAGE

1. *General* (State as specifically as possible the expressions, ideas, etc., which your child appeared to understand through lipreading in natural situations.)
2. *Specific*
   Nouns (Objects-Pictures)
   Commands (Action verbs)
   Color
   Number

233

Verbs
Other adjectives
Adverbs
Pronouns
Prepositions
Conjunctions
Sentences
Phrases
Questions
Stories

PARENT'S REMARKS (Difficulties, cooperation and attitude
of the child, suggestions, etc.)

_____
Teacher

_____

Note—This report to be submitted to teacher on parent's observation and teaching day, and discussed during consultation period.

_____

PARENT'S WEEKLY OBSERVATION REPORT

Child _____ Parent _____

Date _____.

Note—Different aspects of the nursery school training will be
observed and recorded by the parent from week to week. Each
parent should receive guidance and experience in observing and
recording:

(a) a number of children in the same situation (for example,
the lipreading situation);

(b) ten or fifteen minute running records of a number of
children, recording everything that the individual child
does within that period of time; (Plate XXV)

Photo by Ross Madden   Courtesy John Tracy Clinic

PLATE XXV.—Records of everything the young deaf child does are important.

(c) the activities, behavior, attitudes, responses, etc., of a particular child throughout the day in nursery school (at least one other child besides own child).

PARENT'S LESSON PLAN
FOR
PRACTICE TEACHING

(To be submitted to teacher *before* lesson.)

Child_____   Parent_____

Date_____

AIM

SENSE TRAINING
    Materials
    Activity

LIPREADING
    Materials
    Activity

SPEECH
    Materials
    Activity

AUDITORY TRAINING
    Materials, equipment
    Activity

236

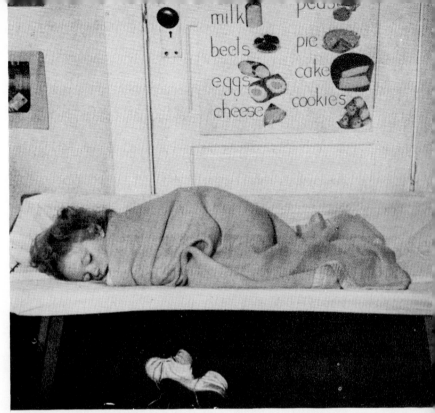

PLATE XXVI.—The afternoon nap for the young deaf child is just as necessary as speech and lipreading.

(*Note*—After the parent has taught a child, she would report on what was done. Very often the planned lesson does not materialize.)

PARENT'S REPORT ON LESSON

(To be completed and submitted after the lesson has been taught. Discussion in the consultation period.)

Child_____   Parent_____

Date_____

SENSE TRAINING

Activity—Response and Attitude

LIPREADING

Activity—Response and Attitude

SPEECH

Activity—Response and Attitude—Intelligibility

AUDITORY TRAINING

Activity—Response and Attitude

WHAT YOU FEEL WAS ACCOMPLISHED

_____

Note—Other records are necessary in relation to the development and progress of the child in other activities such as eating, sleeping, toileting, creative activities, etc. (Plates XXVI and XXVII)

Photo by Ross Madden   *Courtesy John Tracy Clinic*

PLATE XXVII.—Lunchtime for deaf children in Nursery School.

CHAPTER 18

Excerpts from Records

The brief excerpts below are *not* presented merely to show what the young deaf child may accomplish in vocabulary, language skills, etc. They are meant to be of help to parents in understanding that the personality of the individual child largely determines the way he will respond to a particular situation. Parents are inclined to feel discouraged when their child does not "settle down" and perform in the way that some other child does, or in some way that would be more acceptable to them, the parents. Unfortunately, too many parents become so concerned with expediency, or with set standards of behavior and results, that they lose sight of the child and of what *their* feelings and behavior may be doing to him.

Many times, the parent and the teacher have to give time and thought and action to "clearing away the underbrush" in the child's personality before he is ready emotionally to accept direct guidance in specially designed activities. Some of the reactions of the child which disturb the parent are normal; others may be indications of deep problems which will demand months of guidance and readjustment for both parents and child.

LARRY

Larry was three years and two days old when he entered nursery school. His favorite activity was playing in the sandbox. He would cover himself with sand, run trucks through the sand, tear up sand hills, accompanying each of these activities with loud yells and squeals. Indoors, he would crawl over and under tables, turn chairs upside down, remove objects from shelves and shove them around the floor.

Any arbitrary attempts to "make" the child conform to more conventional standards of behavior would have resulted in equally unfavorable reactions: temper tantrums, passive resistance, etc. It was found necessary to give special attention to the parents, while, in the meantime, trying to redirect Larry's energies.

One day, after Larry had done a very thorough job of making the room as untidy as possible, he ran to the children's lockers near the front door and climbed upon them. He began to poke and pull at the very colorful curtains behind the lockers. The teacher casually reached for some color cards. She pointed to the red cherries on the curtain, to the red in Larry's sweater, to the red in her blouse, and to the red card. "They're all red, Larry. That's red, and that's red, and that's red, and that's red. Red, red, red." Larry laughed and very vigorously poked each article with all his three-year-old strength.

Then the teacher pointed to the yellow in the curtains and to the yellow wall. Larry grabbed the cards, pulled the yellow one out, slammed it down on the locker and yelled, "Yayaya." He seemed to enjoy this activity, and went through the various cards matching the colors to corresponding colors within his reach. Each time, he pounded the object of a particular color; he would laugh at the teacher and use his voice in trying to say something, which might have been intended for the color name.

In the days that followed, Larry continued to use voice, but in a more controlled way, and to watch more quietly. Nevertheless, the learning process in the individual periods during the first few months was a most active one, and the teacher had to be prepared to follow Larry. As the months went by, and as the parents received help, Larry's behavior, although still very active, became healthier, and lipreading and speech began to make a favorable impression upon him.

The months of following Larry through his gymnastics were not wasted. His use of voice remained spontaneous and natural. At the end of that first year in nursery school, Larry was imitating the names of all the colors, and several nouns and verbs. His lipreading vocabulary and general language understanding had broadened. There was every indication that he liked to learn. The channeling of his energies by the guidance given to him and his parents required several months, but, in every respect, the time proved to have been well spent.

MOLLY

Molly was a three-year-old who had had some home training before entering nursery school. It soon became apparent that the previous training had been well managed by the parents. Molly was relaxed and cooperative in most situations, with the exception of auditory training. She refused to have anything to do with earphones for the first two months.

Before the family had discovered the real cause of the child's delay in speech development, she had been taken from specialist to specialist, and had been subjected to so many tests that any sustained contact with any part of her head caused an immediate and violent reaction by her.

Although no attempt was made to force earphones upon the child, steps were taken to help her overcome her fear of the equipment and training. The teacher tried the well-known method of wearing the earphones herself as a means of encouraging Molly to wear them. This met with failure.

One day, Molly came in to the training room with another child. The teacher proceeded to do some work on gross sounds with Jane, the other child. No earphones were used. Molly watched quietly, with her hands over her ears. By the time the

242

third sound was introduced, Molly was over at the table trying to knock down blocks with Jane.

For some time, Molly's interest was primarily in the blocks. Before long, she accepted the idea of waiting until she "heard" a sound before knocking over a block. It seemed evident that Molly possessed some residual hearing, but for weeks after she was able to discriminate between two of the gross sounds, she continued to refuse to wear earphones.

Each day for three weeks Molly was allowed to come in with another child who would wear earphones, and finally she put on a pair for a few seconds. The next time she kept them on a little longer. The first listening experiences included music and some favorite stories.

Seven months after entering nursery school, Molly was very enthusiastic about auditory training. She had some usable hearing, and a systematic program was set up for her, whereby lipreading and speech were combined as much as possible with daily auditory training.

Any other than a gradual, unforced, approach to auditory training for a child like Molly would have failed. As it was, Molly was trained to use what hearing she possessed, and was saying whole words intelligibly by her fourth birthday.

AUDREY

Audrey was a three-year-old who showed little interest in the activities of the other children. If she participated at all with other children, it was with older ones. In the training situation, she showed no interest in form boards, toys, etc. She wanted dolls, a doll carriage, the ironing board, etc. It was clear that parent and teacher would have to reach Audrey through her chosen interests.

The teacher set up a housekeeping corner which could be dismantled easily and which might also be used by some of the older children. A small table, a chair, a set of dishes, two dolls with identical clothes, and pairs of toys were a part of the equipment. Through the use of these materials, matching was introduced and carried out. If Audrey chose a red hat for one doll, she or the teacher would find a red hat for the other doll. Blue cups were matched to blue, blue doll shoes to blue ones, etc. If one doll were given a puzzle, the other would have a puzzle. Audrey would do a puzzle for one doll, then one for the other doll. If one doll were given three balls, the other would have three; and each doll would be given a number picture card for three to go with the objects.

By the end of that year, Audrey had developed a very impressive lipreading vocabulary connected with objects and activities of special interest to her, and about other objects and activities in which she had begun to develop interest. Being allowed to explore her special interest, to the extent she needed to explore, resulted in a broadening of her interests.

MIKE

Mike entered nursery school at two years and eleven months. His mother had begun his training at home, and Mike was able to do a large number of sense training exercises and had established an impressive lipreading vocabulary. The teachers noticed Mike's extraordinary capabilities in sense training and lipreading. But they also noticed that, in the speech preparation situations, his voice was strained and unnatural and his whole body became tense as soon as he tried to imitate speech.

Because of this obvious tension, the parents were strongly advised to refrain from "teaching speech" to Mike at home, and give more attention to his activities in the play situation.

During the painting period, he would take his completed page, look around furtively, then tear and mutilate the page until it was a crumpled, sodden mass. When he successfully completed a puzzle, he would throw it in the air, laugh hilariously, and then look around with a startled expression at the teacher.

In the speech and lipreading situation, however, he conformed to every direction, would be very particular about the order of the cards and objects on the table, and would sit very quietly and stiffly awaiting the next suggestion.

No attempt will be made here to interpret the parent-child relationship, nor the basic causes underlying the child's problems. Suffice it to say that the mother received individual attention and guidance; and Mike was given complete freedom in the nursery school, short of seriously endangering himself or others.

Before long, Mike went to the opposite extreme in the special training situation; and a little later the mother reported that Mike's behavior at home was as "bad" as it was at school. It took the parents some time to accept such behavior from their child, and to accept the teacher's acceptance of such behavior. For a while, things seemed to get worse instead of better. Now, when he used his voice, there was no question about its being spontaneous. He would yell and jump and often, during the rest hour, he would be heard babbling freely.

Approximately six months after the parents and child began to receive attention in the nursery school, Mike began to be more relaxed and spontaneous in the special training situation, and more controlled and relaxed in the play and expressive activities. His voice was less strained, and his lipreading, which had been outstanding, continued to improve.

The following statements taken from the running records written by a parent during observation of Mike may help to tell the story of the change in Mike.

October 26. . . . Mike sat in the sandbox, making hills of sand. When he finished each hill, he punched it. Billy came and sat beside Mike. Mike looked around carefully, then pushed Billy to the sand and ran to the swing. Miss—— went over to the swing. When Mike saw her, he "ducked" his head. Then when he saw the teacher smiling, he held up his hands to be lifted into the swing.

January 12. . . . Mike stood watching Danny and Laura playing on the teeter-totter. He picked up a toy truck, ran over to the teeter, and hammered the truck on the board until the wheels broke off. Then he took the pieces over to the teacher, showed them to her, threw them on the ground, and kicked them.

March 18. . . . Mike was going up and down the slide with one of the other children. He saw Miss——— coming out with some puzzles and cards. He poked Billy and pointed to Miss——— as he babbled and chattered. Both children ran to the box on which the puzzles were being spread. Mike pointed to the ball from one puzzle, and said, "Baw," for *ball.* He took Billy's hand, placed it on his (Mike's) cheek and repeated the word. Then he patted Billy on the shoulder when he (Billy) said the word. Then he took Billy's hand, and both children ran to the wagon.

Close observation of Mike and his parents during the following two years showed that the child's most serious problems had been dealt with successfully through the combined efforts of home and nursery school.

———————

Teachers and parents of deaf children have contributed a great deal to the progress of society through their cooperative efforts. The guidance of the young deaf child presents many problematical situations. Many a parent has felt puzzled in spite of the guidance available to her, has wondered if she is walking up a blind alley. A problem seems to be solved, and then suddenly it may seem farther away than ever from solution. The parent of the deaf child does not stand alone in this; the educator often feels the same way. Indeed, the parents and educators who have the moral courage to admit that they do not have all the answers are clearing a swath in the forest of problems created by deafness. In the meantime, parents and teachers have the privilege of working together in leading the young deaf child to oral communication.

Bibliography

1. Ackerman, M. W., "Constructive and Destructive Tendencies in Children: an Experimental Study," *American Journal of Orthopsychiatry*, 8:265-85, 1938.
2. Adams, S., "Analysis of Verb Forms in the Speech of Young Children and Their Relation to the Language Learning Process," *Journal of Experimental Education*, 7:141, 1938.
3. Aldrich, A. and M. Aldrich, *Babies Are Human Beings*. New York: Macmillan Co.; 1942.
4. Alexander, F., *Fundamentals of Psychoanalysis*. New York: W. W. Norton & Co.; 1948.
5. Amen, E. A., "Individual Differences in Apperceptive Reactions: a Study of the Responses of Preschool Children to Pictures," *Genetic Psychology Monographs*, 23:319-85, 1941.
6. Anderson, H. H. and H. Brewer, "Studies of Teachers' Classroom Personalities: Dominative and Socially Integrative Behavior of Kindergarten Teachers," *Applied Psychology Monographs*, No. 6, 1945.
7. Anderson, J. E., "The Development of Motor, Linguistic and Intellectual Skills in Young Children," *Child Development*, 144-74, 1929.
8. ——, *Happy Childhood*. New York: Appleton-Century; 1939.
9. Appel, M. H., "Aggressive Behavior of Nursery School Children and Adult Procedures in Dealing With Such Behavior," *Jour. Exper. Ed.*, 11:185-199, 1942.
10. Arnold, T., *Education of the Deaf*. Farrar Edition, London; 1923. Distributed in America by the Volta Bureau, Washington, D. C.
11. Avery, C. A., "The Social Competence of Preschool Acoustically Handicapped Children," *Volta Review*, June, 1948.

12. Bach, G. R., "Young Children's Play Fantasies," *Psychological Monographs*, No. 2, 59:111-69, 1945.

13. Baker, H. J., *Introduction to Exceptional Children*. New York: Macmillan Co.; 1944.

14. Ballard F., "What Children Like to Draw," *Journal of Experimental Pediatrics*, 2:127-29, 1913.

15. Barker, R. G., B. A. Wright, and M. R. Gonick, *Adjustment to Physical Handicap and Illness: A Survey of the Social Psychology of Physique and Disability*. New York: Social Science Research Council, 230 Park Avenue, Bulletin 55, 1944.

16. Baruch, D. W., "An Experiment With Language Expression in Nursery School," *Childhood Education*, 139, 1931.

17. ——, "A Study of the Reported Tension in Interparental Relationships as Co-Existent With Behavior Adjustment in Young Children,"*Jour. of Exper. Ed.*, 6:187-204, 1937.

18. ——, "Doll Play in Preschool as an Aid in Understanding the Child," *Mental Hygiene*, 24:566-77, 1940.

19. ——, *New Ways in Discipline*, New York: McGraw-Hill Book Co., Inc., 1949.

20. Bell, A. G., *The Mechanism of Speech*. New York: Funk and Wagnalls; 1916.

21. Bender, L., and A. Woltman, "The Use of Plastic Material as a Psychiatric Approach to Emotional Problems in Children," *Am. Jour. of Orthopsych.*, 7:283-300, 1937.

22. —— and ——, "The Use of Puppet Shows as a Psychotherapeutic Method for Behavior Problems in Children," *Am. Jour. of Orthopsych.*, 6:341-54, 1936.

23. Bennett, R., *The Play Way of Speech Training*. London: Evans Bros., Ltd.; 1935.

24. Berry, G., "Use and Effectiveness of Hearing Aids," *Laryngoscope*, 49:912-924, 1939.

25. Berry, M. and J. Eisenson, *The Defective in Speech*. New York: Appleton-Century Co.; 1942.

26. Betts, E. A., *The Prevention and Correction of Reading Difficulties*. Evanston, Illinois: Peterson & Co.; 1935.

27. Biber, B., "Children's Drawings: From Lines to Pictures," *Bureau of Educational Experiments*, New York; 1934.

28. Blatz, W. E., *Understanding the Young Child*. New York: Morrow & Co.; 1944.

29. Bodycomb, M., "The Speech of the Deaf and of the Normal Speaker," *Volta Review*, November, 1946.

30. Borden, R. C., and A. C. Busse, *Speech Correction*. New York: Crofts & Co.; 1937.

31. Braley, K., J. Utley, and E. Harris, "Some Aspects of Acoustic Work," *Volta Review*, June, 1938.

32. Bruhn, M. E., *The Muller-Walle Method of Lipreading for the Deaf. (Bruhn Lip Reading System).* Lynn, Massachusetts: The Nichols Press; 1929.

33. Brunschwig, L., "A Study of Some Personality Aspects of Deaf Children," *Teachers College Contribution to Education*, No. 687, New York, 1936.

34. Bryan, C. E., "An Experimental Study of the Dramatization of Family Life Situations by Young Children," unpublished master's thesis, The University of Minnesota; 1940.

35. Buell, E. M., *Outline of Language for Deaf Children, Bk. I.* New York: Lexington School for the Deaf; 1934.

36. —, "Word Pictures," *Volta Review*, June, 1926.

37. Bunch, C. C., *Clinical Audiometry*. St. Louis: C. V. Mosby Co.; 1943.

38. Bunger, A. M., *Speech Reading — Jena Method.* Ypsilanti, Michigan: The Author: 1932.

39. Carhart, R., "Selection of Hearing Aids," *Archives of Otolaryngology*, 535 N. Dearborn St., Chicago 10, Illinois, July, 1946.

40. Carmichael, L., Editor, *Manual of Child Psychology*. New York: J. Wiley & Sons, Inc.; 1946.

41. Champney, H., "The Measurement of Parent Behavior," *Child Development*, 12: 131-66, 1941a.

42. —, "The Variables of Parent Behavior," *Journal of Abnormal and Social Psychology*. 36:525-42, 1941b.

43. Cockrell, D., "Design in the Paintings of Young Children," *School Arts Magazine*, 30:33-39; 112-119, 1930.

44. Cole, E., "Language Problems and Children," *Hygeia*, 21:301, 1943.

45. Conn, J. H., "The Child Reveals Himself Through Play: the Method of Play Interview," *Mental Hygiene*, 23:49-70 1939.

46. Curti, M. W., *Child Psychology*. New York: Longmans, Green & Co.; 1940.

47. Davis A. W., "Fantasy Life of Deaf Children," unpublished master's thesis, Syracuse University, 1930.

48. Davis, H., Editor, *Hearing and Deafness*. New York: Murray-Hill Books, Inc.; 1947.

49. DeLemos, P., *The Art Teacher*. Worcester, Massachusetts: The Davis Press; 1930.

50. Despert, J. L., "A Method for the Study of Personality Reactions in Preschool Age Children by Means of Analysis of Their Play," *Journal of Psychology*, 9:17-29, 1940.

51. Division of Child Development and Teacher Personnel (Staff of), *Helping Teachers Understand Children*. Washington, D. C.: American Council on Education; 1945.

52. Doerfler, L. G., "Neurophysiological Clues to Auditory Acuity," *Journal of Speech and Hearing Disorders*, 13:227-232, 1948.

53. English, O. S., and G. H. J. Pearson, *Emotional Problems of Living*. New York: W. W. Norton & Co., Inc.; 1945.

54. Erickson, E. H., "Studies in the Interpretation of Play. Clinical Observation of Play Descriptions in Young Children," *Genetic Psychology Monographs*, 22:557-671, 1940.

55. Ewing, I. R., *Lipreading and Hearing Aids*. Manchester: Manchester University Press; 1944.

56. ——, "Eleanor Has Made History. What Next?" *Volta Review*, April, 1948.

57. —— and A. W. G. Ewing, *The Handicap of Deafness*. London: Longmans Green & Co.; 1939. (Volta Bureau, Washington, D. C.)

58. —— and ——, *Opportunity and The Deaf Child*. London: University of London Press Ltd.; 1947. (Volta Bureau, Washington, D. C.)

59. Fletcher, H., "The Science of Hearing," *Volta Review*, August, 1948.

60. Ford, C., "Language for Deaf Children in Primary and Junior Grades," unpublished curriculum, Ontario School for the Deaf, Belleville, Ontario; 1939.

61. ——, "Teaching Language to Children Born Deaf," *Special Class Teacher*, November, 1946.

62. Foster, C. J., *The Attractive Child*. New York: Julian Messner Inc.; 1941.

63. Frank, L. K., "The Fundamental Needs of the Child," *Mental Hygiene*, 20:353-79, 1938.

64. ——, "The Problem of Child Development," *Child Development*, 6:7-18, 1935.

65. ——, "The Reorientation of Education to the Promotion of Mental Hygiene," *Mental Hygiene*, 23:529-43, 1939.

66. ——, "Projective Methods for the Study of Personality," *Journal of Psychology*, 8:389-413, 1939.

67. Freud, A., "Introduction to the Technique of Child Analysis," *Nervous and Mental Diseases Monograph Series*, 1928.

68. Freud, S., "A Child Is Beaten," *Selected Papers*, New York, 1920.

69. Froechels, E., *Psychological Elements in Speech*. Boston: Expression Co.; 1932.

70. ——, *Speech Therapy*. Boston: Expression Co.; 1933.

71. Gates, A. I., *The Improvement of Reading*. New York: Macmillan Co.; 1937.

72. Gesell, A., "Normal and Deaf Children in the Preschool Years," *Volta Review*, November, 1946.

73. ——, *Infant and Child in the Culture of Today*. New York: Macmillan Co.; 1942.

74. ——, *The First Five Years of Life*. New York: Macmillan Co.; 1940.

75. Goldstein, M., *The Acoustic Method for the Training of the Deaf and Hard-Of-Hearing Child*. St. Louis: The Laryngoscope Press; 1937.

76. ——, *Problems of the Deaf*. St. Louis: The Laryngoscope Press; 1933.

77. Goodenough, F. L., *Anger in Young Children*. Minneapolis: University of Minnesota Press; 1931.

78. ——, "Use of Pronouns by Young Children," *Journal of Genetic Psychology*, 52:333, 1938.

79. Goodman, M., "Language Development in a Nursery School Child," *Child Research Clinical Seminar* 2, #4, 1936.

80. Gordon, A., "Speech for the Deaf Child," *Special Education Review*, June, 1948.

81. Gottemoller, R., "The Influence of Certain Aspects of the Home Environment on the Adjustment of Children to Kindergarten," *Smith College Studies in Social Work*, 9:303-59, 1939.

82. Gray, G. W., and C. M. Wise, *The Bases of Speech*. New York: Harpers; 1934.

83. Gray, W., M. Monroe, and L. Gray, *The Basic Readers—Pre-Primer Program*. Teachers' Edition. New York: Scott, Foresman & Co.; 1941.

84. Gregory, I., "A Comparison of Certain Personality Traits and In-

terests in Deaf and in Hearing Children," *Child Development*, 9:277-280, 1938.

85. Groht, M., "The Teaching of Language," *Volta Review*, November, 1946.

86. Gruenberg, S. M., *We, The Parents*. New York: Harpers; 1939.

87. ——, *Your Child, Today and Tomorrow*. Philadelphia: Lippincott Co.; 1934.

88. Guilder, R. P., and L. A. Schall, "Rehabilitation of the Child Who is Handicapped by Deafness," *The Laryngoscope*, October, 1944.

89. ——, and L. A. Hopkins, "The Small Deaf Child During Preschool Years," *Volta Review*, January, 1936 (Reprint #440).

90. ——, and ——, "Program for the Testing and Training of Auditory Function in the Small Deaf Child During Preschool Years," *Volta Review*, January and February, 1935.

91. Guthrie, V. S., "Creative and Expressive Activities for Young Deaf Children," *Volta Review*, December, 1945 and January, 1946.

92. ——, "History of Nursery School Education for the Deaf," *Volta Review*, January and February, 1945.

93. Hanford, H. E., *Parents Can Learn*. New York: Holt & Co., 1940.

94. Harley, C. W., "Art in the Nursery School," *Progressive Education*, 8:570-575, 1931.

95. Harris, G., "An Acoustic Training Program for Severely Deaf Children," *Volta Review*, October and December, 1946, and January, 1947.

96. Hattwick, B. W., "Inter-relations Between the Preschool Child's Behavior and Certain Factors in the Home," *Child Development*, 7:200-26, 1936.

97. ——, and M. Stowell, "The Relation of Parental Overattentiveness to Children's Work Habits and Social Adjustments in Kindergarten and the First Six Grades of School," *Journal of Education Research*, 30:169-76, 1936.

98. Haycock, S., *The Teaching of Speech*. Washington, D.C.: Volta Bureau; 1941.

99. Hirsch, D., "Advice to Parents, Guardians and Teachers, Concerning the Education of Deaf-Mutes," *American Annals of the Deaf*, 22:93-103, 1877.

100. Hudgins, C. V., "A Rationale for Acoustic Training," *Volta Review*, September, 1948.

101. ——, "Speech Breathing and Speech Intelligibility," *Volta Review*, November, 1946.

102. Isaacs, S., *Intellectual Growth in Young Children*. New York: Harcourt, Brace & Co.; 1930.

103. ——, *Social Development in Young Children*. New York: Harcourt, Brace & Co.; 1933.

104. ——, *The Nursery Years*. New York: Vanguard Press; 1938.

105. Johnson, H. M., *The Art of Block Building*. New York: John Day Co.; 1933.

106. Johnson, W., and Associates, *Speech Handicapped School Children*. New York: Harpers; 1948.

107. Kantner, C. E., and R. West, *Phonetics*. New York: Harpers; 1941.

108. Kawin, E., *The Wise Choice of Toys*. Chicago: University of Chicago Press; 1938.

109. Keaster, J., "A Quantitative Method of Testing the Hearing of Young Children," *Journal of Speech and Hearing Disorders,* 12:159-160, 1948.

110. Kent, M., *Suggestions for Teaching Rhythm to the Deaf*. Maryland: School for the Deaf; 1938.

111. Kimmins, C. W., *Children's Dreams*. New York: Longmans Green & Co.; 1920.

112. Knight, M., "Emotions of Young Children," *Volta Review*, 44:69-72, 1942.

113. ——, "A Descriptive Comparison of Markedly Aggressive and Submissive Children," *Smith College Studies in Social Work*, 1:93, 1933.

114. Korner, F. K., *Hostility in Young Children*. New York: Grune & Stratton, 1949.

115. Landreth, C., *Education of the Young Child. A Nursery School Manual*. New York: J. Wiley & Sons, Inc.; 1942.

116. Lane, H. S., "Education of the Deaf Child," in *Twentieth Century Voice Correction*. Edited by E. Froechels, Philosophical Library Inc., 15 E. 40th St., New York; 1948.

117. ——, "Influence of Nursery School Education on School Achievement," *Volta Review*, 44:677-681, 1942.

118. Larsen, L. L., "Recordings for Auditory Training," *Volta Review*, September, 1949.

119. Lassman, G. H., "Lipreading in Nursery School," *Volta Review*, September, 1948. Reprint #605.

120. ——, "Parent Participation in Teaching Speech to the Deaf Child," *Journal of Speech and Hearing Disorders*, 13:366-368, 1948.

121. ——, and H. Montague, "The Deaf Baby," *Volta Review*, July, 1949.

122. —— and ——, "Hearing Aids and Young Deaf Children," *Volta Review,* September and October, 1949.

123. Levine, E. S., "Psychological Sidelights," *Volta Review,* January, 1948.

124. Lillywhite, H., "Organizing a Speech Clinic in a Small College," *Journal of Speech and Hearing Disorders,* 13:264-267, 1948.

125. Lippitt, R., "An Experimental Study of Authoritarian and Democratic Group Atmospheres," in *Studies in Topological and Vector Psychology I,* University of Iowa Studies in Child Welfare, 16:No.3, 1940.

126. Love, J. K., and J. R. Van Meter, "The Deaf Child," *Journal of Exceptional Children,* November, 1945.

127. Lukens, H., "A Study of Children's Drawings in Early Years," *Pediatrics Seminar,* 4:79-110, 1896.

128. McCarthy, D., "A Comparison of Children's Language in Different Situations and Its Relation to Personality Traits," *Journal of Genetic Psychology,* 36:583, 1939.

129. McCormick, H. W., *Acoustically Handicapped Children.* New York: City Board of Education; 1941.

130. McFarlane, J. W., "Family Influences on Children's Personality Development," *Childhood Education,* 15:55-58, 1938.

131. Meltzer, H., "Children's Attitudes to Parents," *Am. Jour. of Orthopsych.,* 5:244-65, 1938.

132. Menninger, K. A., *The Human Mind.* New York: A. A. Knopf; 1946.

133. ——, "The Mental Effects of Deafness," *Volta Review,* 25:439-445, 1923.

134. Meyers, C., "The Effect of Conflicting Authority on the Child," in *Studies in Topological and Vector Psychology III,* University of Iowa Studies in Child Welfare, 20:1944.

135. Montague, H., Editor, *Correspondence Course for Parents of Preschool Deaf and Hard-of-Hearing Children.* John Tracy Clinic, 924 W. 37th St., Los Angeles 7, California; Revised, 1948.

136. ——, "Letters to the Mother of a Deaf-Born Child," *Volta Review,* October, 1942.

137. ——, "What the Otologist Should Know About the Educational Problems of the Deaf," *The Laryngoscope,* June, 1946.

138. ——, "Hearing Aids for Deaf Children," *Volta Review,* March, 1946. Reprint #571.

139. ——, "Home Training for Preschool Deaf Children Through Cor-

1espondence," *Journal of Speech and Hearing Disorders*, 14: 131-134, 1949.

140. Morley, D. E., "Rationalism in Testing the Hearing of Children," *Volta Review*, 50:468-476, 1948.

141. Murchison, C., Editor, *Handbook of Child Psychology.* Worcester: Davis Press; 1931.

142. Myklebust, H. R., "Clinical Psychology and Children With Impaired Hearing," *Volta Review*, February, 1948.

143. Nelson, B., "The Essentials of Acoustic Programs," *The American Annals of the Deaf*, May, 1942.

144. Nemoy-Davis, *Correction of Defective Speech Sounds.* Boston: Expression Co.; 1937.

145. New, M. C., "Speech for the Young Deaf Child," *Volta Review*, October, 1940. Reprint #511.

146. ——, "Color in Speech Teaching," *Volta Review*, March and April, 1942. Reprint #518.

147. ——, "The Nursery School," *Volta Review*, November, 1946.

148. ——, "Speech in Our Schools for the Deaf," *Volta Review*, February, 1949.

149. Newell, H. W., "Psycho-Dynamics of Maternal Rejection," *Am. Jour. of Orthopsych.*, 4:387-403, 1934.

150. ——, "A Further Study of Maternal Rejection," *Am. Jour. of Orthopsych.*, 6:576-607, 1934.

151. Nielson, D. V., "Gay, Profitable Rhythm Classes," *Volta Review*, January, 1948.

152. Nitchie, E. B., *Lipreading Principles and Practice.* Philadelphia: Lippincott Co.; Revised Edition, 1946.

153. Numbers, F. C., "Is Speech Teaching a Failure?" *Volta Review*, May, 1946.

154. Numbers, M. E., "Using the Hearing of Children So Deaf That They Entered School Speechless," *Volta Review*, March, 1937.

155. ——, "What Training Should Be Required By the Teacher?" *Volta Review*, November, 1938.

156. ——, and C. V. Hudgins, "Speech Perception in Present Day Education for Deaf Children," *Volta Review*, 50:449-456, 1948.

157. O'Connor, C. D., "Acoustic Training in the Curriculum," *Volta Review*, May, 1936.

158. ——, "What Every Superintendent of a School for the Deaf Should Know About Hearing Aids and Their Uses," *Volta Review*, November, 1938.

159. ——, "How Our Schools Can Solve Some of Today's Problems," *Volta Review,* September, 1948.

160. Olney, E., and H. Cushing, "A Brief Report of the Responses of Preschool Children to Commercially Available Pictorial Materials," *Child Development,* 6:52-55, 1935.

161. O'Neil, J. M., Editor, *Foundations of Speech.* New York: Prentice-Hall, Inc.; 1941.

162. O'Shea, M. V., "Some Aspects of Drawing," *Educational Review,* 14:263-84, 1897.

163. Panel of Educators, "Nursery and Preschool," *Volta Review,* September, 1948.

164. ——, "Education of Young Deaf Children—The Advisability of Residential Nursery Schools," *Volta Review,* September, 1946.

165. Parents' Committee, "A Parent Guide on Comic Books," *California Parent-Teacher,* September, 1948.

166. Parents' Discussion, "The Parents Discuss Young Deaf Children Going to Boarding School," *Volta Review,* December, 1946.

167. Peck, A. W., E. E. Samuelson, and A. Lehman, *Ears and the Man.* Philadelphia: F. A. Davis Co.; 1926.

168. Pennington, J., *The Importance of Being Rhythmic.* New York: G. P. Putnam's Sons; 1925.

169. Perrine, V. D., *Let the Child Draw.* New York: F. A. Stokes Co.; 1936.

170. Phillips, W. C., and H. G. Rowell, *Your Hearing and How to Preserve It.* New York: D. Appleton & Co.; 1932.

171. Piaget, J., *The Language and Thought of the Child.* New York: Harcourt, Brace & Co.; 1926.

172. ——, *The Moral Judgment of the Child.* New York: Harcourt, Brace & Co.; 1932.

173. ——, *The Child's Conception of the World.* New York: Harcourt, Brace & Co.; 1926.

174. Plant, J. S., "Mental Hygiene Aspects of Problems of the Deaf," in *Proceedings of the International Congress on the Education of the Deaf,* 9:464-474, 1933.

175. Pugh, G. S., "Appraisal of Silent Reading Abilities of Acoustically Handicapped Children," *Volta Review,* April, 1946.

176. Rand, W., M. Sweeny and E. L. Vincent, *Growth and Development of the Young Child.* Philadelphia: Saunders Co.; 1940.

177. Read, K. H., "Teachers' Verbal Contacts With Children," *Peabody Journal of Education,* 18:No.5, 1941.

178. Report of a Committee From the American Association to Promote

the Teaching of Speech to the Deaf, "The Home and the School for the Deaf," *Volta Review,* March, 1946.

179. Rogers, C., *Counseling and Psychotherapy.* New York: Houghton Mifflin Co.; 1942.

180. Rooney, A. G., "Parent Education—Emphasis on the Preschool," *Volta Review,* December, 1946.

181. Rowell, H. G., "Deafness in Children," *Parents' Magazine,* 5:20-1. 1930.

182. ——, *Hear Better.* New York: Funk & Wagnalls Co.; 1937.

183. Russell L. E., "Beginning Lipreading," *Volta Review,* October, 1940. Reprint #507.

184. Sapir, E., *Language.* New York: Harcourt, Brace & Co.; 1921.

185. Seth, G. and D. Guthrie, *Speech in Childhood.* New York: Harcourt, Brace & Co.; 1935.

186. Shaw, R. F., *Finger Painting.* Boston: Little, Brown & Co.; 1934.

187. Silverman, S. R., and S. G. Taylor, "The Choice and Use of Hearing Aids," in *Hearing and Deafness.* See Bibliography #48.

188. ——, "Training for Optimum Use of Hearing Aids," *The Laryngoscope,* 54:29-36, 1944.

189. Slavson, S. R., Editor, *The Practice of Group Therapy.* New York: International University Press; 1947.

190. Small, A., "The Deaf Child At Home," *Volta Review,* October, 1942.

191. Smith, A., "Parent Education and Group Therapy," *Journal of Clinical Psychology,* 4:214-217, 1948.

192. Springer, N. N., "A Comparative Study of Behavior Traits in Deaf and Hard-of-Hearing Children of New York City," *American Annals of the Deaf,* 83:255-273, 1938.

193. ——, "A Comparative Study of Psychoneurotic Responses of Deaf and Hearing Children," *Journal of Educational Psychology,* 29: 459-466, 1938.

194. ——, "A Further Study of the Psychoneurotic Responses of Deaf and Hearing Children," *Jour. of Educ. Psych.,* 29:590-596, 1938.

195. Staff of Junior High School 47, "A New Approach to the Education of Two- and Three-Year-Old Deaf Children," *Volta Review,* May, 1949.

196. Staff of the Child Study Association of America, *Parents Questions.* New York: Harpers; 1936.

197. Stalmaker, E., "Language of the Preschool Child," *Child Development,* 4:229, 1933.

198. Stoddard, G. D., "The Planning and Equipping of Nursery Schools," *American School and University*, 7:218-222, 1935.

199. Stoner, M., "What the Inexperienced Teacher Needs in the Way of Supervision," *Volta Review*, November, 1946.

200. Stott, L., "Some Family Life Patterns and Their Relation to Personality Development in Children," *Jour. of Exper. Ed.*, 8:148-60, 1939.

201. Symonds, P. M., *The Psychology of Parent-Child Relationships*. New York: Appleton-Century Co.; 1939.

202. Thom, D. A., *Every Day Problems of the Every Day Child*. New York: Appleton-Century Co.; 1942.

203. Thonssen, L., and E. Fatherson (compiled by), *Bibliography of Speech Education*. New York: H. W. Wilson Co.; 1940.

204. Thorn, A., *Music for Young Children*. New York: Scribner's Sons; 1929.

205. Tracy, L., "Suggestions to the Parents of Deaf and Hard-of-Hearing Children," Pamphlet, *John Tracy Clinic*, Los Angeles, California.

206. Travis, L., and D. Baruch, *Personal Problems of Everyday Life*. New York: Appleton-Century Co.; 1941.

207. Uden, A. V., "Music and Dancing for the Deaf," *Volta Review*, August, 1949.

208. Updegraff, R., "Recent Approaches to the Study of the Preschool Child. Influence of Parent Attitudes on Child Behavior," *Journal of Consulting Psychology*, 3:34-36, 1939.

209. Utley, J., "A Test for Lipreading Ability," *Journal of Speech Disorders*, 11:109-116, 1946.

210. Washburn, R. W., *Children Have Their Reasons*. New York: Appleton-Century Co.; 1942.

211. Waterman, E., *The Rhythm Book*. New York: A. S. Barnes & Co.; 1936.

212. Whitehouse, L., "A Spokane Christmas Card," *Volta Review*, January, 1948.

213. Whitehurst, M. W., *Train Your Hearing*. Washington, D. C.: Volta Bureau; 1947.

214. ——, *Auditory Training for Children*. New York 21: Hearing Rehabilitation Centre, 654 Madison Avenue; 1949.

215. Wilde, P., "Racketeering in Hearing Aids," *The American Mercury*, August, 1948.

216. Wile, I. S., "Some Mental Hygiene Problems of the Deaf," in *Pro-*

ceedings of the International Congress on the Education of the Deaf, 464-474, 1933.

217. Winston, M. E., "What the Parent Can Do for the Preschool Deaf Child," *Volta Review,* October, 1933. Reprint #429.

218. Witmer, H. L., "Parental Behavior as an Index to the Probable Outcome of Treatment in a Child Guidance Clinic," *Am. Jour. of Orthopsych.,* 3:431-444, 1933.

219. Wolf, A., *The Parents' Manual.* New York: Simon and Schuster; 1941.

220. Wolff, W., *The Personality of the Preschool Child.* New York: Grune and Stratton; 1947.

221. Wood, G., "Art in the Daily Life of the Child," *Child Welfare Pamphlet* #73, Iowa City: University of Iowa Press; 1939.

222. Wood, K. W., "The Parents' Role in the Clinical Program," *Journal of Speech and Hearing Disorders,* 13:209-210, 1948.

223. Wright, J. D., *The Little Deaf Child.* (out of print—Volta Bureau Library.)

Index